To Blair,

Thank you

you made on

of humility o

Much love,

Raphael

(re)DISCOVERING
The MINISTRY of the EVANGELIST

(re)DISCOVERING

The MINISTRY of the EVANGELIST

RAPHAEL ANZENBERGER

(re)Discovering the Ministry of the Evangelist

Published by
Anzenberger Ministries Ltd
216 Stone Crop Rd
Wilmington, DE 19810-1320

ISBN 978-0-9863348-0-1 softcover
ISBN 978-0-9863348-1-8 ePub
ISBN 978-0-9863348-2-5 MOBI

Translated from French by Lori Varak
Cover design by Jeff Gifford
Interior design by Beth Shagene

Printed in the United States of America.

2014—First edition

To Abigail, my daughter
You are the joy of your father,
And your zeal for the Gospel puts me to shame.
May this book encourage you to excel as an evangelist!

Table of Contents

ACKNOWLEDGEMENTS

This book is, for the most part, the fruit of my doctoral thesis at Columbia International University. For this reason, I would like to begin by thanking those whose generous contributions enabled me to complete my research: the Leighton Ford Ministries Foundation, the Lloyd Trust, and the Zacharias Trust. I'm also grateful to my doctoral supervisor, Roy King, and committee members Martin Sanders and Mike Barnett, who have encouraged me to publish my work. Many thanks to the International Committee of the Global Evangelists' Forum for their support of this project.

This book is also the story of the evangelists who have deeply influenced my theological understanding and my ministerial practice: My grandmother, Marie-Louise, who courageously preached the Gospel despite adversity; My professor of Evangelization, Bill Jones, who passionately shares his faith with everyone God's puts in his path; My mentor, Leighton Ford, whose vision for global evangelism has impacted the Lausanne Movement; and Ravi Zacharias, who carefully articulates scripture-based thinking in a way that is always relevant to society.

Finally, I am indebted to Alain Stamp for repeatedly reviewing my manuscript, and to all my friends who have contributed to this work (in order of appearance): Emmanuel, Lindsay, Saotra, Florent, and Philippe. Thanks to Lori Varak for her excellent translation to English, Jennifer Williamson for her wise input, and Susanna Cancassi and John Topliff for their amazing editorial work.

This book is also theirs!

INTRODUCTION

WHY DO I NEED AN INSTRUCTION MANUAL?

When I turned thirty, my wife bought me a grill. We had been looking at different models for a couple of years, and Karen finally decided it was time to make a decision. This was the one! It seemed perfect in every way. My mouth watered as I imagined the sizzling hot dogs, pork chops and chicken we would soon be grilling. I was pumped: A Frenchman living the American dream! We had a mobile home on the campus of Columbia International University in South Carolina, and I was driving a BMW (never mind that it belonged to my father-in-law). I was finishing up my degree to become an evangelist while working at the Michelin plant where I was putting into practice what I was learning. I was enjoying every aspect of my life.

It was time for a party! Karen invited almost everyone in the trailer park, as well as a few of my work buddies. I had been studying the Bible with several of them, meeting at McDonalds before the 8 a.m. shift. We set the brand new grill in the middle of the living room for all to see. Of course, at this point, it was still in the box.

As soon as we had polished off the traditional birthday cake, I decided to dive into my new project. My coworkers were just as impatient as I was. We could not wait to fire up the beast! We just needed to put the thing together, and we would be on our way to chowing down on some juicy steaks. You could have cut the tension with a knife. Dozens of different grill parts were strewn across our living room floor, but I quickly sized up the situation. With just a bit of organization, we would have this baby up and running in no time.

I gave my friend Richard the task of managing the work group. Richard had graduated at the top of his class from one of the best engineering schools in France. He was outstanding in his field. I couldn't take any chances; I needed all the odds in my favor. Laurent, another top engineering graduate, would be his assistant. The cream of the crop, the French elite, was all abuzz as they gathered around my new grill.

"Oh this should be easy, I've got another friend who's got the same grill!" said Richard. He sounded pretty sure of himself. "With this model, we need to start at the top."

Always the skeptic in our group of friends, Laurent looked doubtful. He was constantly looking for a way to streamline projects, and this one would be no exception. "I think we'd finish faster if we started with the lower part of the grill."

I was feeling trapped. I needed to make a decision. We would start with the upper portion of the grill.

Karen stuck her head in the living room to let us know that we had thrown the instruction manual away with the box.

Instructions? Who needs instructions? We sure didn't! We knew what we were doing. Instruction manuals are for sissies and women. We possessed an inborn sense of engineering. We knew all we needed to know. After all, we were the French elite, weren't we?

Unfortunately, the grill seemed to have other ideas. The beast would not be tamed! No matter, we would get to the bottom of it in a jiffy. Richard was doing a brilliant job managing the project. Finally, with a sigh of satisfaction, he proclaimed the grill assembled.

"We're done!"

The other guests held their breath in anticipation. He shut the lid… the bottom grill was sticking out.

"This thing's defective!" he cried.

Laurent frowned, "I told you guys we should start with the bottom first."

I noticed that Karen had retrieved the instructions from the box and laid them on a chair near where we were working. You know, just in case.

Frustrated, we started taking the grill apart. Laurent took over this time. Everyone was getting a little bit edgy. Richard was mumbling under his breath, "… junk… made in China… not up to EU standards…" A few minutes later, Laurent breathed a sigh of relief. "We're done!" he said.

He shut the lid. The upper grill was sticking out. This was ridiculous.

We were defeated; the French elite had been humiliated. Karen didn't say anything, she just smiled. I love my wife, she is always right.

(re)Discovering the Ministry of the Evangelist

The book you now hold in your hands is an instruction manual for evangelists. Its goal is to help the budding evangelist grasp the purpose, function and objectives of this often overlooked ministry. This book is also designed for pastors, theologians and church leaders who wish to deepen their understanding of the challenges and joys involved in opening up their institutions to the ministry of the evangelist. Finally, it is a useful tool for those who may be in the midst of developing a training program for evangelists.

The evangelist is a reemerging species. Some people are excited about the possibilities, while others remain skeptical. The latter often have mixed emotions because of their past experience with evangelists. Kind of like the grill that sticks out when you close the lid, evangelists make us nervous. They don't fit our little boxes. Are they "defective" in some way? Probably not. It might be helpful for us to rediscover how God, in his infinite wisdom, ordained this ministry for the building up of the saints. We must never forget that it was God who gave some to the Church "as evangelists" in the first place (Ephesians 4:11).

THEOLOGICAL DISQUALIFICATION?

The word evangelist (*euangelistês*) is only found three times in the New Testament:

- Philip the evangelist is mentioned in Acts 21:8
- The evangelist is listed in Ephesians 4:11 as one of the gifts that Christ gave to the Church
- Paul exhorts his protégé in 2 Timothy 4:5 to do the work of an evangelist.

Friedrich Gerhard observes: "Except in ecclesiastical literature this is a rare word. In a non-Christian sense it is attested only on a poorly preserved inscription, from Rhodes, IG, XII, 1, 675, 6, where it means 'one who proclaims oracular sayings.'"[1] The fact that the evangelist is mentioned only a few times in the New Testament could lead one to believe that this ministry has become obsolete, or at best, secondary in importance. Jacques Buchhold reminds us that "Ephesians 4:11-12 is also the only passage in the epistles of the New Testament that uses the word 'pastor' to refer to Church leaders [...] though no one doubts the importance of a pastor's role in a Christian community!"[2]

But why is the term *euangelistês* not observed more often in the Scriptures?

> The word "evangelist" occurs three times in the New Testament. Based on the timing of these occurrences,

[1]Friedrich Herhard, *Theological Dictionary of the New Testament* (Grand Rapids: Eerdmans, 1964), 736.

[2]Jacques Buchhold, "Evangéliste," in *Dictionnaire de Théologie Pratique* (Charols: Excelsis, 2011), 383. (free trans.)

> we can conclude that the word was introduced into the language of mission at a late stage. We are still in a position to see what the motive for its introduction was, for, at a time when the term "apostle" had already come to be applied to a particular and clearly defined circle of pioneers of mission, those outside that circle who had a similar office of preaching were termed "evangelists". The difference between "apostle" and "evangelist" is not one of function. It is rather that the latter term reflects a later period, say, the second or third generation, by which time the "apostle" has become either in the Lucan sense a figure in the *Heilsgeschichte* itself or in the deutero-Pauline sense an authoritative first link in the chain of tradition.[3]

Well, that clears things up a little bit. So, since there is no theological reason for us to reject the ministry of the evangelist, we can continue with our rediscovery!

WHAT IS AN EVANGELIST?

An evangelist is someone who proclaims, preaches and spreads the Gospel, especially the Good News of Jesus Christ. While it is true that the word *euangelistês* appears only three times in the New Testament, we find the verb *euangelizomai* (to evangelize) over 50 times. Thus, we learn that Jesus was an evangelist, because he preached the Good News (Luke 20:1). Paul practiced the ministry of the evangelist (Romans 1:15), as well as Philip, who was also a deacon (Acts 21:8), and Timothy, a pastor (2 Timothy 4:5). The apostles and their early

[3]Werner Kramer, *Christ, Lord, Son of God* (Naperville: Allenson, 1966), 55.

converts were all evangelists, since "those who were scattered went about preaching the word" (Acts 8:4). An evangelist proclaims the Good News of Jesus Christ and invites his hearers to place their trust in him. He is engaged in a two-way activity which flows outward (from the Church towards those outside of the Church), as well as inward (those who repent and move in towards the Church). This action is carried out by men and women who have been gifted by the Holy Spirit to bring the lost to repentance and salvation.

Smith summarizes the ministry of the evangelist like this:

> An evangelist according to the Bible is a man qualified by God to speak his name and his power to those who are outside the fold of Christ, and bring them to acknowledge the saving power of the Gospel, believe it, and become members of the body of the redeemed.[4]

ARE WE ALL EVANGELISTS?

The connection between the ministry of the evangelist and the role of the evangelist is clear in the New Testament.[5] Simply put, the evangelist champions the cause of evangelism in the Church. To put things into perspective, if theologians are particularly interested in helping the Church better understand Scriptures, if pastors are particularly passionate about equipping the Church for works of service and care,

---

[4]Alfredo Smith, "The Evangelist and a Torn World: We Are Called by God," in *The Work of an Evangelist* (Minneapolis: World Wide Publications, 1983), 152.

[5]For further reflection on the word *euangelizomai,* read the article (in French) by Jacques Buchhold, "La Nature du ministère d'évangéliste dans le Nouveau Testament," in *Dictionnaire de Théologie Pratique,* 384.

evangelists are particularly concerned that the whole Church takes the whole Gospel to the whole world.[6]

Therefore not all are evangelists. Yet we are all called to give testimony to our faith. The apostle Peter encourages us to "honor Christ the Lord as holy, always being prepared to make a defense to anyone who asks you for a reason for the hope that is in you; yet do it with gentleness and respect" (1 Peter 3:15). Paul exhorts us in the same manner: "Let your speech always be gracious, seasoned with salt, so that you may know how you ought to answer each person" (Colossians 4:6). In other words, we are all called to be witnesses, but some witnesses are specifically called to be evangelists.

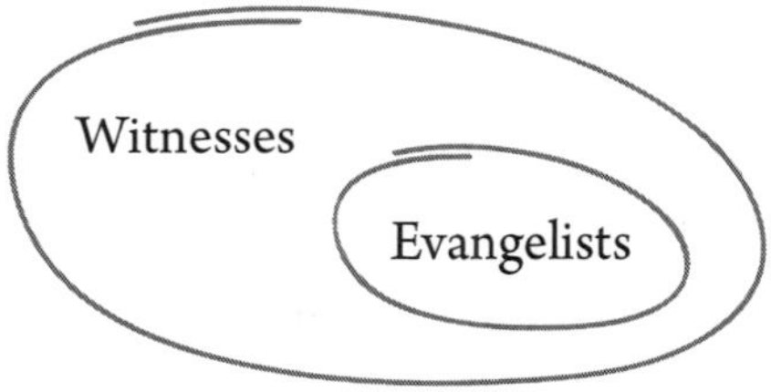

GOD IS AT WORK!

This book bears the mark of evangelists who minister throughout the French-speaking world. It is the fruit of more than ten years of personal theological consideration as well as numerous conversations with my coworkers in Europe, Canada, and Africa.

God loves to surprise us. Back in 2005, during the National Consultation on Evangelism held in Lyon, France,

[6]Cf. The Lausanne Covenant

we realized that there were only a handful of evangelists still hanging on, doing their best to share the Good News. Five years later, more than two hundred evangelists met in the same building for the 4th Annual European Evangelist's Forum[7]. One-third of those attending were under the age of 25. Europe is waking up to evangelism. We see the same thing happening in Quebec, where over three hundred men and women recently attended the Canadian Evangelist's Forum. Western Africa, Central Africa, and the Caribbean are also getting in on the action… the entire French-speaking world is being set on fire by the desire to see souls saved. God loves to surprise us. But some peoples' reactions to the ministry of the evangelist are just as surprising:

Do we really need to get back to the ministry of the evangelist – isn't it kind of old-fashioned?

Isn't an evangelist simply an assistant pastor who lacks theological training?

If we encourage the ministry of the evangelist, will we discourage individual Christians from sharing their faith?

The grills are sticking out. The top grill and the bottom grill. We can't get the lid down; what are we going to do? Not to worry, God is watching. The instruction manual is right over there on the chair. The question is are we willing to use it?

---

[7]The Global Evangelists Forum is a platform for reflection, training and facilitation for evangelists, in association with biblical training institutes, church fellowships, missions and other Christian organizations which promote evangelism. URL: www.globalevangelistsforum.org

CHAPTER 1

ARE WE ALL BILLY GRAHAMS?

The same ministry expressed in different ways

Quick, what's the first thing you think of when I say the word evangelist?

BEWARE OF STEREOTYPES!

Wherever I teach, whether it's in Europe, North America or Africa, the first person that most people think of is Billy Graham. He is the universal symbol of all evangelists.

I have always wanted to meet Billy Graham. Kind of like how some people dream of going to the Vatican to meet the Pope. I went to America hoping to meet him but have never yet had the privilege of shaking his hand. Whenever I talk to Blair Carlson, who organized all of the campaigns for Mr. Graham as he calls him, my admiration continues to grow.

One day, I asked Blair to share with me the greatest secret he had ever learned from this man of God, and he said, "Preach the Gospel, brother! Preach the Gospel!"

That, in a nutshell, describes the passion behind the man. After he preached, Billy Graham always asked Blair "Was I faithful to the biblical message? Did I preach the Gospel in its entirety?" It's almost disturbing to imagine an evangelist with so many years of experience who is still so concerned with whether or not he was faithful to the Scriptures!

The apostle Paul was also an evangelist, and we are reminded of his words: "For Christ did not send me to baptize but to preach the gospel, and not with words of eloquent wisdom, lest the cross of Christ be emptied of its power. For the word of the cross is folly to those who are perishing, but to us who are being saved it is the power of God" (1 Corinthians 1:17, 18). It is my daily prayer that I would stay true to the Gospel, and I thank you, Mr. Graham, for your example.

If Billy Graham is the prime example of an evangelist, does that mean that all Christians are called to be itinerant preachers? Though the message stays the same, I believe that there are different ways to deliver it.

SEVEN KINDS OF EVANGELISTS

During the National Consultation on Evangelism in 2005, my colleague and good friend Emmanuel Maennlein suggested seven different kinds of evangelists.[1] We see examples of these lived out everywhere we go.

---

[1]In His infinite wisdom, God can also modify the ministry of an evangelist, or make them move from one expression to another.

1. The preacher evangelist

Today, we would probably list Billy Graham, Stephen Lungu, Luis Palau, Becky Pippert and others under this category. The preacher evangelist preaches the Gospel. It is his reason for living. He even preaches the Gospel in his sleep (I know this to be true, having slept in the same room as Emmanuel Maennlein several times!)

The preacher evangelist revs up when his feet hit the platform. The bigger the crowd, the faster his heart beats. He has barely started his message and he is already thinking about the altar call! He prepares the message in the silence of his office, but his goal is to share it with the multitudes. This is the paradox of the preacher evangelist. He is alone in the midst of a crowd.

The preacher, more than anyone else, must have a solid message. A good theological background accompanied by a healthy dose of homiletics is strongly recommended. He also needs to be able to spiritually discern the heart motivation of those who ask to see him privately after the message. He learns and perfects these facets of his ministry over time and by experience.

The strengths of the preacher evangelist: Mass evangelism! The preacher has the privilege of speaking to large groups, and the joy of seeing people come to Christ on a regular basis. His newsletters buzz with wonderful testimonies of salvation. What a blessing to see tens, hundreds, even thousands of men and women responding to the message of the Gospel with his own eyes! What a blessing, and at the same time, what a huge responsibility!

The challenges of the preacher evangelist: Solitude. The preacher often travels alone. It is usually harder to deal with the post preaching than with the pre-preaching. The preacher evangelist finds himself alone in his hotel room, physically and emotionally exhausted. He struggles with his darkest thoughts. Somewhere between pride and humility, the preacher must apply his message to his own life, and come back to the cross to lay down any glory he may have taken for himself.

2. The artist evangelist

The artist evangelist uses the arts to communicate the Gospel, be it through music, drawing or live painting. With so many different mediums available to illustrate the message of the Good News, we must be careful to remember the difference between the role of the artist evangelist and that of a Christian artist – it is not the same thing. Each has its place, but the artist evangelist uses his art as a platform for preaching the Gospel. His art is only the means to an end, which is communicating the message.

The artist evangelist is a talented person. He's an artist! Enough said. He doesn't just wake up one day and proclaim himself an artist. He knows that his art is a God-given gift, a talent that must be honed, it's who he is. God is an artist, he is also a poet. Paul reminds us that "we are his workmanship [*poiema*], created in Christ Jesus for good works, which God prepared beforehand, that we should walk in them" (Ephesians 2:10). God understands the artist evangelist like no one else!

The strengths of the artist evangelist: His art! The artist-evangelist is known and recognized for the quality of his art. He uses albums, comic books, paintings, whatever he can to get his message across to as many people as possible! He can also use his art to support humanitarian causes. For example, French musician Pierre Lachat has decided to associate his music with Compassion International to encourage people to sponsor children in third-world countries. Another musician, Philippe Decourroux, uses his concerts to speak to people about human trafficking.

The challenges of the artist evangelist: His art! An artist can set a week aside to write a new song, but find himself days later still sitting in front of a blank page. "Lord, give me inspiration! And hurry!" The artist is in a constant battle with himself and the urgent need to come up with new ideas from deep within the well of his own creativity.

Art may be an extremely effective tool for communicating the Gospel to the masses, but it needs to be done well if it is to be appreciated by the public. That's not an easy task! The artist evangelist often makes a living from what he does, which means a huge investment of his time and money, without any guarantee of success. The artist evangelist can be tempted to allow his art to become the goal instead of a tool for communicating the Gospel. The cross can get lost in the art, the call to repentance more vague as time goes by, to avoid offending the non-believers in the crowd. The evangelist can be swallowed up by the artist.

One negative element the artist evangelist may run into is criticism. Newcomers love to share their opinion on anything and everything, and our churches are full of people like that. "I preferred your old style, I feel like you've taken a step in the wrong direction. But that's just my opinion…" Gulp!

3. The church planter evangelist

You might be surprised to find the church planter included under the heading "evangelist." I understand where you are coming from. Classic missiologists like me tend to distinguish the evangelistic role from the apostolic one, or the evangelist from the church planter. So why are we talking about him in this chapter? Whoever can do more can certainly do less. In other words, a church planter is an evangelist who considers evangelism to be most effective when it is lived out in the community where he lives. He's an evangelist who has undergone a DNA mutation, in a way.

Alan Hirsch[2] explains the difference between the two in the following manner:

	APOSTOLIC	EVANGELISTIC
Missional impact	Extension	Growth
Primary metaphor	Missionary	Messenger
Primary thrust	Missional (go to them)	Attractional (come to us)
Key fruit or sign	Church planting	Soul winning
Their passion	Movements	Conversions
Mathematical growth	Multiplication	Addition

[2]Alan Hirsch and Tim Catchim, *The Permanent Revolution: Apostolic Imagination and Practice for the 21st century Church* (San Francisco: Jossey-Bass Leadership Network Series, 2012), Table 3.1.

	APOSTOLIC	**EVANGELISTIC**
Cultural competency	Multicultural	Monocultural
Cultural orbit	Translocal (glocal)	Supralocal
Constructive role	Architect	Builder
How they are often viewed by the institution	As agitator for development	As asset for growth
Focus / perspective	Macro / systemic	Micro / personal
What they feel called to	Nations (translocal)	Local and regional (supralocal)
What it initiates	Ventures	Relationships

Differences between Apostolic and Evangelistic Ministries

I can already hear your reactions: Either "I agree 100%!" or "You don't know what you're talking about!" Although the two ministries may have some differences, many similarities remain. They both recognize the need to get the job done.

The apostle Paul was a church planter extraordinaire (it's not very often that we see a church planted in just two weeks, as he did in Philippi). But he was also an amazing evangelist. The point where these two ministries converged was the culture in which Paul lived. A church planter must be in sync with the people who live in the community where he hopes to start a church. He can surround himself with evangelists, but he must set the example! The church planter must do the work of an evangelist and then some. Where the evangelist sees souls to save, the church planter sees a church which must be planted.

My analysis differs from Hirsch's in the area of the

evangelist's influence. He limits it to the translocal sphere, in other words, to the geographic and sociological sphere of the home church. But what about the example of Philip in the Bible? He crossed social (Acts 8:26-40), cultural (Acts 6:1-6; 21:8) and religious (Acts 8:5-13) boundaries. His ministry may have been limited to Judea, geographically speaking, but his vision was for the nations! His ministry was, therefore, both transcultural and supralocal – just like Billy Graham's.

The strengths of the church planter evangelist: The church plant! What a joy to witness the fruit of one's ministry growing into a local church, a community of men and women united through the Spirit by Christ's death on the cross, in an intimate relationship with the Father. The Church is a reflection of the Trinity! United in diversity, one in community.

The challenges of the church planter-evangelist: The church plant! Once the work is done, one of two things often happens in the life of the church planter. Either he stays around too long and fails to pass the leadership of the church on to those who should have it, or he decides to take an early retirement. Church planting demands a colossal investment on the part of those involved, the church planter and his family. I believe it's possible to successfully plant one, maybe two churches during one's career. But three? Very unlikely!

4. The street evangelist

They're always there. Rain or shine, you can count on them to be around. You will find them preaching wherever and whenever possible, outside the train station, witnessing door-to-door in an apartment building, giving away Bibles at a stand in the open air market or taking surveys on the beach. These evangelists always have a smile on their faces and a Bible or a tract in their pockets, ready to share their faith with whomever they come across. These guys are my heroes, there's no one more courageous than they are! They are zealous and have a tenacity that I really admire. They know the field, and they love it!

Who says we don't need street evangelists anymore in the 21st century? Those of us who are comfortably ensconced behind our church walls? If so, we must stop! Ulrich Parzany said, "God is multifaceted! Each different facet of evangelism is a sign of divine creativity. Who are we to disqualify a certain facet simply because it doesn't meet up with our standards? Do we know better than God?" I remember back in 2005, just after a colleague of mine spoke to us, I was sitting between two evangelists who were arguing about the subject:

"No one does evangelism like that anymore, it's old-fashioned!"

"Are you kidding?" cried the other one. "It's the only method that works!"

God is multifaceted.

The street evangelist loves being out in the field. He lives for it. Where others would be petrified at the idea of sharing with a hostile crowd, the street evangelist's heart is filled with divine courage as he imagines an extraordinary opportunity to share the Gospel. It's a mystery! I remember when my friend Philippe was leading an evangelistic camp in the streets of Saint-Etienne. Street surveys were definitely his thing. The rest of the team was exhausted; they'd been out on the street for hours and were ready to head back to camp for dinner.

Philippe was doing a survey with a passer-by: "It's the last one," he said. We finally had to drag him off the street, practically kicking and screaming. "Just one more! Just one more!" That's the street evangelist's heartbeat: "Just one more! I'll give up my dinner to talk to just one more person!"

The strengths of the street evangelist: His love for the field and his amazing ability to enter into contact with people. Recently I was in Geneva, Switzerland, with my friend David. I was fascinated by his ability to create situations where he could talk to people about his life and his faith, just by playing his musical instrument. For him it was as easy as it would be for you or me to talk to a neighbor about the weather. It was bewildering, yet refreshing at the same time. The street evangelist is also an amazing motivator. He isn't satisfied to head out alone; he wants everyone to share his joy in speaking to others about God.

The challenges of the street evangelist: He doesn't understand why everyone else isn't doing the same thing he is. It really bugs him. He tends to get frustrated when, after sharing for the umpteenth time with his home church, "... it's still the same two or three people who come out to witness with us on Saturday afternoon! If the church wants a revival, they need to get out on the streets!" Street evangelism is an art, and it's not for everyone. But the rest of us need to know how to encourage those who are called to it!

5. The social worker evangelist

If you ever attended a Christian camp when you were young, you have probably come into contact with this type of evangelist. He may even be the person who led you to Christ using a puppet show or magic tricks. If you have ever been in prison (which I sincerely hope is not the case for your sake), you have probably met at least one social worker evangelist. Maybe he even came into the confines of your cell to share some words of hope with you. You finally knew what it meant to be free... in Christ!

Their ministries are intended for a certain section of the population: Children, teens, business people, urban youth, the elderly, prisoners, and addicts. All of these groups have specific needs, and the social worker evangelist is trained to meet them where they are.

This type of evangelist has a burden for his specific target group. Where does that burden come from? First and foremost it comes from God. It also comes from his background, his social environment. He defends his ministry in the name of justice and fairness: everyone has a right to know that God loves them and wants them to have a relationship with Him! You will find that the social worker evangelist has often followed a rigorous course of studies to get to where he is today, and his ministry is performed in a professional manner. He is not into improvisation. This is very important because the authorities tend to keep an eye on this type of person and a lack of professionalism could jeopardize his ministry. But when the social worker evangelist knows what he's doing and he does it well, his audience is happy and there's no problem!

The strengths of the social worker evangelist: his professionalism. That's the driving force behind a job well done, and it often guarantees that his ministry will bear much fruit. I remember an evangelist who worked with street children in

Romania and decided to organize a meeting for the kids... in the middle of the town square. I was shaking in my boots! On top of choosing to meet in the most obvious place possible, he was bringing in the heavy artillery. He set up a sound system and a puppet stage, and donned a red nose as he invited the children to attend. I feared for his life and mine as well! But I was pleasantly surprised to see the children enchanted and the parents challenged in their own beliefs. (I know, I'm a man of little faith... I'm working on it!) One mother approached me: "You've been playing with our children for two hours and no one has gotten into a fight yet. How do you do it?" Ah, the power of the Gospel presented by an evangelist who knows what he's doing... there's nothing like it!

The challenges of the social worker evangelist: the challenge of succession. Oftentimes, the social worker evangelist gets so wrapped up in his ministry and his pursuit of excellence that he forgets the importance of passing the torch on to the younger generation of evangelists. Because he is concerned with the quality of his ministry, he may become overly cautious. This is understandable, but it can quickly turn into a sort of exclusivity, and that is a shame. These evangelists often began their ministry alone; they have gotten used to carrying on alone in the long term. But they need to remember that God is the one who opens doors to any ministry (cf. Colossians 4:3).

6. The apologetics evangelist

His speech is complicated, he's always quoting different authors, he's interested in philosophy and cosmology; he buys books, reads books, sleeps with books. He's the apologetics evangelist, the defender of the Christian faith. He uses apologetics, which is a discipline normally reserved for the dogma department, to share the Good News. We think of Ravi Zacharias, John Lennox or Alister McGrath in this category. He certainly has a head full of knowledge, but he also has a heart that burns for the Gospel. It's a rare combination, but very effective for sharing the truth of God's Word with intellectuals, as well as the masses.

Apologetics evangelists have marked church history. Men like Justin Martyr, Irenaeus of Lyon, Origen, St. Augustine, Thomas Aquinas, Blaise Pascal, Soren Kierkegaard, Newbigin, Schaeffer and Van Til. These human legends have been the driving force behind so many different schools of apologetic reasoning. They were the source of theories such as evidentialism, presuppositionalism, existentialism and many others. Some apologetics evangelists specialize in a specific field of knowledge, such as epistemology or the correlations between faith and science; others are more generalized in their thinking. In any case, these evangelists possess a deep well of knowledge, all the while keeping in mind that the cross is folly for the world, and that true wisdom is to know the Father and His Son, by the renewing of the mind through the Spirit.

Apologetics evangelists are always on the alert. Like the Native Americans who put their ears to the ground to listen for invaders, these evangelists have their ear tuned to what is happening in society. They are acutely aware that philosophical trends always hit the arts before being accepted at the heart of society. They analyze currents in culture and sound the alarm when danger approaches: "Beware! Ultra-modernism, relativism, pluralism on the horizon!" As soon as they perceive a current trend which attacks the foundations of their faith, they are on the warpath, publishing papers containing their rebuttals. They will use any available medium to get their message out: Books, television shows, podcasts, conferences or blogs. These are just some of the possible channels used to communicate the message of the Gospel and to "make a defense to anyone who asks [them] for a reason for the hope that is in [them]" (1 Peter 3:15).

The strengths of the apologetics evangelist: His expertise! He has a vast range of understanding. He is knowledgeable in so many areas and seems to have an answer for everything – fascinating! He proves to the average Christian that believing in God isn't the same thing as "receiving the gift of stupidity" as my friend Michael Ramsden would say, and that our faith can stand up to the test of scrutiny. We don't need to set aside our scientific beliefs or our concern for historical accuracy.

Yes, our Christian faith is coherent! The apologetics evangelist goes into the local church to train believers and provide them with the necessary means to share the hope that is in them and to expand their witness in their own sphere of influence. That way, when a coworker says, "I'd like to believe, but..." the Christian is equipped to give an answer, or at least be able to offer him a book where he will find the answers himself.[3]

The challenges of the apologetics evangelist: Pride! He's an intelligent guy. His command of philosophy and his

[3]Raphaël Anzenberger, *Moi aussi je voudrais croire, mais...* (I'd like to believe, but...) (Marpent: BLF, 2008), 96 pages.

love for rhetoric can lead him to believe that even the Gospel might need a little help on his part in order to be better suited to the intellectual crowd. When he starts thinking that way, he has fallen into Satan's trap. The Gospel is the power of salvation for all who believe, it doesn't need any help from us. It is powerful enough without the apologetics evangelist's improvements.

7. The soul winner evangelist

Put this guy in front of a crowd and he panics. But get him in a one-on-one situation with a non-Christian at a café table, or underneath a mango tree, and he is another person! The soul winner evangelist likes to go fishing, one soul at a time. His strength is found in his persistence. If you are a non-believer, there's no use trying to resist! This evangelist communicates a deep love for others and his faith is contagious. This soul winner is gifted in the art of apologetic conversation. He knows what questions to ask, and when to ask them: "Do you know God, or are you still looking? Would you like to know Him?" He's a wonderful mix of steamroller and charm, and he's irresistible.

I am privileged to have a soul winner evangelist on my church planting team. Within a few months of moving to our town, she had already led four people to the Lord and baptized two of them. I admit it's a little bit frustrating for the rest of team, but at the same time it's so refreshing.

The strengths of the soul winner evangelist: His contagious faith. He is a great example of faith in action. As the unbeliever watches him live, he realizes that Christianity is not simply a philosophical choice, but a transformed life. A few questions here and there, a personalized Bible study, an invitation to make a decision and before you know it the person is making a decision for Christ. What a joy!

The challenges of the soul winner evangelist: The best way to paralyze a soul winner is to give him too many responsibilities in the church, even as the leader of the evangelization committee. It's a double whammy: You have taken your best agent off the field and you've given him a responsibility that doesn't fall within his gift mix. The result? An evangelism team that can't do its job and a frustrated soul-winner!

IN CONCLUSION

Edward Bounds, theologian and fervent man of prayer, liked to say: "The church is looking for better methods; God is looking for better men."[4] It's so true!

In order for evangelism to become a reality, God raises up evangelists. But in order for that same evangelism to touch the hearts of all different kinds of people, God raises up different types of evangelists. God is multifaceted!

[4]Edward Bounds, *The Complete Works of E. M. Bounds on Prayer* (Grand Rapids: Baker Books, 2000), 447.

DIGGING DEEPER

Interview with **Emmanuel Maennlein,**
Evangelist, conference speaker and author

What are some of the new methods of evangelism that you've noticed recently?

In the past ten years, I think there's been a new emphasis on internet evangelism. If you listen to guys like Eric Célérier and others, you'll see what I'm talking about. These guys are great examples of this new and innovative type of evangelism. They are the Billy Graham and Luis Palaus of the 21st century via the internet. They realized the amazing potential of this form of communication before anyone else did. Thanks to websites like KnowingGod.com and others, tens of thousands of men and women have discovered and accepted Jesus Christ as their Savior. As I've traveled in different contexts, I've actually met people who made a decision for Christ through one of these websites.

I think that the main style of evangelism that we're going to see developing over the next few years will be anything that has to do with the audio-visual world. This is a must in today's media, and there are no limits to what can be done with it.

Another trend that I've observed is anything that has to do with street performances. Youth for Christ, for example, is doing an amazing job with their summer camps on the beach, and in the city of Mulhouse, with their *Bouge ta ville* ("Move your city") campaigns. Street evangelism allows you to be in direct contact with people and their questions, their hopes and their needs. The Gospel is truly lived out in this type of evangelism, and new evangelists are encouraged to use their gifts.

What do you think about the new internet evangelists? Is this another form of evangelism that we should add to the mix?

Yes, I think it's another legitimate kind of evangelist, and a good one at that. Who doesn't use the internet today? Even senior citizens are surfing the net! This is why we need internet evangelists. There's still so much to do if we want to touch everyone with the Gospel. There is room for all different types of evangelists who, with the help of the Holy Spirit, will find open doors and ideas which will impact their peers with the message of the cross.

How would you encourage someone who is trying to discover his or her style of evangelism?

I would tell them four things:

1. **Listen:** What is your heart telling you? What makes your heart beat faster? What is your passion? What motivates you beyond anything else? What is your reason for living? What is it that makes you want to get involved in this particular kind of evangelism?
2. **Think about what the Holy Spirit is telling you:** He's the one you depend on as an evangelist. What is God communicating to you as you pray and seek his face concerning your ministry? What talents and spiritual gifts has he given you?

3. **Seek the counsel of others:** Watch how other gifted people express their ministry. Meet with them; ask them questions. Listen to what they have to say and learn from their wisdom. Allow yourself to be inspired by their experiences, their struggles, their faith, etc.
4. **And finally, practice, practice, practice:** The advice that I would give to any budding evangelist is this: Take hold of every opportunity to share your faith. For example, if you are a preaching evangelist, say yes to any and all invitations you receive to share the Gospel. Don't wait until you're standing in front of a crowd of thousands or in a sold-out stadium. If you do, you may never get the chance to speak! No matter how many people you're preaching to, where you are, what the circumstances are, what the weather conditions are, how prepared you feel or where your emotions are at any given moment: go for it! Preach with all your heart and soul – even if there are only five or ten people listening, and only one of them is not yet a Christian. Be faithful in your ministry and God will do amazing things through you.

What, in your opinion, do all these different styles of evangelists have in common?

I can think of two things right off the bat:

1. The evangelist has a heart for lost people. That's the main thing that all evangelists have in common, no matter what their style is. Some people may find that a bit simplistic, and maybe it is. But it sure works for him. All of the evangelist's prayers, thoughts, energy and projects are centered on men and women who do not yet know the Gospel. This passion is what drives them, and they must

be careful to keep the flame alive. They must remember that their God-given ministry depends largely on this enthusiasm.

2. The evangelist's main priority is to share the Gospel. Philip the evangelist is a great example of this. The Bible describes him as a man who "proclaimed… Christ" (Acts 8:5). Ulrich Parzany characterizes the ministry of an evangelist with two intentional limitations: a message limited to the basics of the Gospel and an audience limited to non-believers. God did not call or equip the evangelist to simply wax poetic, to share deep philosophical truths, or to teach a class, but to preach the glorious Gospel of Jesus Christ in the power of the Holy Spirit. This is when God's anointing becomes obvious in the evangelist's ministry. Thus, hearts are touched and lives are transformed.

CHAPTER 2

WHO ME? AN EVANGELIST?

Qualifications for ministry

I remember it like it was yesterday. It was a beautiful day in May. Yves Perrier, a well-known French evangelist, had been invited to speak at the Sunday morning service in my church. Before he handed the microphone over to Yves, the worship leader asked him this question: "Yves, what are France Evangelization's most pressing needs today?"

Yves thought for a moment, and then he said, "If you had asked me that question ten years ago, I would have told you that we need money to finance our evangelistic campaigns. But today I look around, and there is no one behind me to take over when I'm gone. What France Evangelization needs today is a new generation of evangelists!"

As I sat there in the church, I felt the Spirit of God poke me on the shoulder to say, "That's for you. Sign up!" That was in 1994.

Ten years passed between God's call on my life and the beginning of my ministry. After several years in Africa, then in the States, I was chomping at the bit to meet the movers and shakers of evangelism in the French-speaking world.

I remember one such meeting with an evangelical leader. I laid out my heart regarding my vision for the ministry of the evangelist. After a few minutes, I sensed that I wasn't getting anywhere, when he looked me in the eye and said, "You say you're an evangelist, but I don't know you from Adam. How do I know what you say is true? Can you show me any fruit from your ministry?" I realized I was back in France where no one sugar coats anything! That was in 2004.

GOD IS STILL CALLING EVANGELISTS TODAY

I am so thankful for the prayers of those who have gone before me. I believe that God has answered above and beyond what they asked. The next generation is here and they're ready to take up where Yves left off! We see it in our Global Evangelist's Forums, on the beaches during the Plage Station campaigns, and in our Emerging Evangelist Network (R2E) program. Generation Y (those born between 1979 and 2004) is ready to step up to the bat, and it is awesome! Guys and girls whose hearts burn for the Lord. Now it's up to us to accompany them in their mission!

These young people that God is raising up are not only French – they are European, African, Asian, American... international! In 2006, over six hundred young leaders with a heart for evangelism met in Malaysia for the Younger Leaders Gathering of the Lausanne Movement.[1] What energy! After

[1]http://www.lausanne.org

Europe and North America, emerging countries are stepping up for world evangelization. The statistical center of gravity of global Christianity is now solidly anchored in the African continent. If you could take a picture from heaven, you might be surprised to learn that the average Christian is any color but white, and speaks anything but English!

The 3rd Annual Lausanne Congress on World Evangelization was held in Cape Town, South Africa in November of 2010.[2] It was amazing to observe the missionary zeal of the young people from the African continent, more than half of whom were age 25 or under.

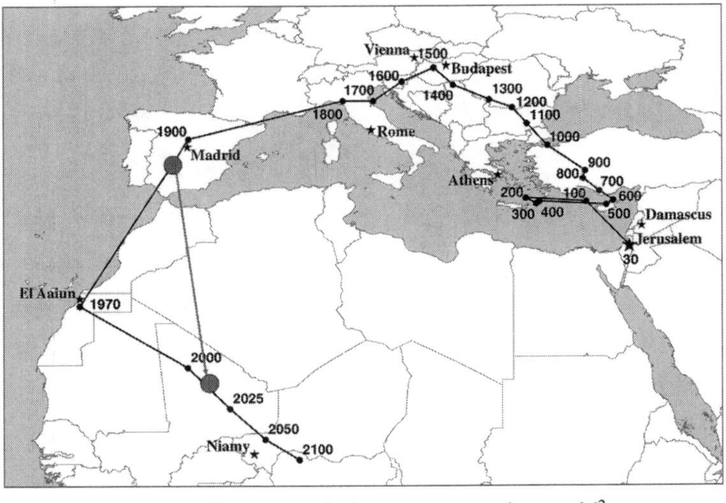

Center of gravity of Christianity in the world[3]

[2]The Lausanne Movement, *The Cape Town Commitment.*

[3]Todd Johnson, "World Christian Trends," *Lausanne World Pulse.* Speech given during a conference at the biannual meeting of Lausanne International Leadership, Budapest (Hungary), June 18-22 2007. Edited in August 2007. URL: http://www.lausanneworldpulse.com/766/08-2007?pg=all (last consulted September 2, 2013)

In order to encourage this generational renewal and be a part of the new order of world evangelization, we must be clear as to what we expect from the young evangelists that God brings to our door. That is the goal of this book. But in order to do that, we first need to answer the question: Who qualifies for this ministry? And that is the goal for this chapter. Because, if everyone is an evangelist, as some people maintain, then no one really is. But, if it's true that some are specifically gifted as evangelists, then we better know how to recognize them!

THREE QUALIFICATIONS FOR THE MINISTRY OF THE EVANGELIST

Before we go any further, we need to clarify some biblical vocabulary. The apostle Paul reminds us: "But grace was given to each one of us according to the measure of Christ's gift. Therefore it says, "When he ascended on high he led a host of captives, and he gave gifts [*domata*] to men." [...] And he gave the apostles, the prophets, the evangelists, the shepherds and teachers, to equip the saints for the work of ministry, for building up the body of Christ" (Ephesians 4:7-12).

Jesus Christ gave gifts to men: *Domata,* men and women[4] chosen by a sovereign God for the building up of His Church. Jacques Buchhold reminds us that "in giving the apostles, prophets, evangelists and pastor-doctors to His church, Jesus gave the gift of persons, setting them apart from the other 'gifts' (*charismata*) that He gave to His people (see the list

[4]Consider the brilliant female evangelists like Jeanne Saillens, Mady Vaillant, Anne Graham Lotz, Joni Eareckson Tada or Lacey Nicole Sturm from the group Flyleaf.

of gifts in 1 Corinthians 12:28-30), thus emphasizing their importance."[5]

We need to make a preliminary distinction between the functions (*domata*) mentioned in Ephesians 4 and 1 Corinthians 12:28 and the gifts of the Spirit (*charismata*) that we find in the rest of Scripture.

We'll look more closely at the second distinction later on in the book; the difference between the function and the office (see Chapter 6). What we need to keep in mind for now is that certain people (*domata*) have received a specific call to ministry. They have been set apart by Jesus Christ for the good of his Church.

How do I know if I am one of these *domata*? Do I need to receive a specific call?

If you look at the writings that are available on this subject, you will quickly observe that there are three main qualifications for the ministry of the evangelist: He must be called by God, be confirmed by the local church and possess certain competencies or skills which are specific to the type of evangelistic ministry in view (apologetics, preaching, artistic, etc.).

1. Demonstrating the reality of the call

Have I been called to be an evangelist? Yes, I have, and I remember it like it was yesterday. God calls some people in very clear ways; for others, it may not be quite so obvious. Nonetheless, there is a quiet assurance that he has his hand on your life for a very specific ministry. Ulrich Parzany talks about being "driven by love for God and for the lost,

[5]Buchhold, 384. (free trans.)

and consumed with the desire to preach the Gospel to sinners."[6] "For if I preach the gospel that gives me no ground for boasting. For necessity is laid upon me. Woe to me if I do not preach the gospel!" (1 Corinthians 9:16).

God calls us in different ways. It might be while praying, during an invitation after a message, reading a missionary biography or through the prophetic Word. When we receive God's call, we are filled with fear and excitement at the same time. Fear, because our carefully planned future has suddenly been turned upside down. Excitement because we know without a shadow of a doubt that nothing will ever be the same.

Being called by God doesn't necessarily mean that one's life will change radically, or that his ministry will begin immediately. The apostle Paul was called in the year 33 AD, on the road to Damascus. But it wasn't until twelve years later, in 45 AD, that he began to minister in Antioch under the direction of Barnabas. In my case, ten years passed between the time that God called me to be an evangelist and the actual moment that my ministry began. This is not the norm, but let it be an encouragement to you young evangelists. Things will change ... soon, but you must be patient.

"You say you're an evangelist, but I don't know you from Adam. How do I know what you say is true? Can you show me any fruit from your ministry?" Even though there might have been a kinder way of putting it, there's still a lot of truth in what was said.

Stephen Olford, the great preaching evangelist, insists

[6]Ulrich Parzany, "The gift and calling of the evangelist," in *The Mission of an Evangelist: Amsterdam, 2000,* ed. Douglas, J., 23-30. (Minneapolis: World Wide Publications, 2001), 25.

that the evangelist must be capable of proving, humbly but with confidence, that his ministry does bear fruit. In other words, he must be able to show that a certain number of conversions have come as a result of his ministry.[7]

Does that mean that if someone has never brought anyone to faith, that he or she is not an evangelist? Yes and no. If someone spends their entire life in an evangelistic ministry, without ever seeing someone come to Christ, they may not actually be called to be an evangelist. But if you were called yesterday and haven't yet seen any conversions, don't worry. That's why, in our Emerging Evangelist Network program (R2E), we like to have a blend of young evangelists. Some have already seen more than many conversions in their eighteen years on this earth, while others have yet to lead someone to Christ. If the call is clear, the results will come in time.

2. The affirmation of the local church

When Jesus calls, he always does it in the context of the local church. Paul and Barnabas were called and affirmed by the church in Antioch, who later sent them out as missionaries (Acts 13:3). In other words, the evangelist doesn't send himself out; he is sent by his church.

I always tremble a little bit when I receive an application letter for evangelistic ministry and the person insists that they don't think they need to have any connection with a local church. They often say that Jesus himself was above that kind of requirement. Really? He who is right now building his

[7] Stephen Olford, "The Evangelist's gift and ministry," in *The Work of an Evangelist*, ed. Douglas, J., 143-150 (Minneapolis: World Wide Publications, 1983), 143.

Church would seek people to minister outside of that same Church? That seems strange to me! I can understand an evangelist harassing his pastor because it is not possible to be in a church that does absolutely nothing in evangelism, but to set oneself above the authority of the local church is another thing altogether. If an evangelist does not have a healthy view of the local church, what will he do with the people he leads to the Lord? I'll let you mull that over for a few minutes.

Paul reminded Timothy: "Do not neglect the gift you have, which was given you by prophecy when the council of elders laid their hands on you" (1 Timothy 4:14). Later, he tells him, "For this reason I remind you to fan into flame the gift of God, which is in you through the laying on of my hands" (2 Timothy 1:6). Whose hands sent you? Your own? What a blessing it is when struggles come to be reminded that you have been sent out, that it's not just a mistake in casting, that your call was observed, confirmed and validated by the elders of your local church. That these same hands continue to support and bless you: "Hang in there, we're with you all the way!" So often, evangelists live in isolation. But the self-proclaimed evangelist is like a stray dog without a collar, seeking legitimacy that he never obtained beforehand, because he didn't realize the importance of it. This has to stop! It's not how the Scriptures call us to live. How can we preach the Word if we refuse to submit to the practical aspects of ministry?

Which hands have sent you, my friend? It's such a joy for me to know that as I write these lines, my church is praying for me, morning and night. This book is their book too. Sharing is a part of ministry.

3. Competencies specific to the type of ministry in view

When an evangelist asks to join our preaching ministry, we make sure that he actually possesses certain competencies in that area, even if, in the long run, he has room to grow.

If an artist wants to share the Gospel through an artistic ministry, but has no skill in this area, you can imagine the results. In short, each area of ministry has certain skill requirements.

The following list is not exhaustive, but it gives us a good idea of what we are looking for in ministry skills:

EVANGELISM STYLE	SKILL SET
Preacher	• Preach from a biblical text in the local church • Communicate the Gospel from a specific text to a specific audience • Know the audience • Able to answer objections against himself or his message • Extend an invitation and following it up • Capable of discerning a true from a false conversion • Lead a private discussion with discernment • Help the local church prepare evangelistic events • Adaptable to different types of media • Discerning what is going on in the world around him
Artist	• All of the skills mentioned for the preacher, along with the following: • Obvious artistic skills in his area • Promotion of his specific artistic medium
Church-planter	• All of the skills mentioned for the preacher, along with the following: • Follow people up in their walk with God • Team leader • Manage the different phases of a church plant

EVANGELISM STYLE	SKILL SET
Street-evangelist	• Make contact with people on the street using a specific tool (tracts, surveys, etc.) • Adept at turning the conversation toward spiritual subjects • Persevere through times of "contact famine" and when results are not seen
Social worker	• Professionally trained for the type of ministry in view • Be a good listener • Encourage a biblical view of his profession • Defend vision for ministry • Motivate local churches to get behind the ministry in view
Apologetics	• All of the skills mentioned for the preacher, along with the following: • Good grasp of philosophical concepts • Working knowledge of many different schools of thinking • Develop a form of cultural exegesis • High level of mastery of the language in which he is ministering • Fluency in the different debate techniques
Soul winner	• Manage his time in order to have long periods of time available for in-depth discussions • Ability to take a person from an initial interest in the Gospel through an inductive Bible study • Discern the different steps of a person's spiritual development • Know when to seize the occasion to invite someone to give their life to Christ

There is a certain learning curve specific to each particular type of evangelistic ministry. Mastering the necessary skills for your area of ministry can take time. That is why it is important to be patient and to surround yourself with people who can serve as mentors and lead you through the learning process.

IN CONCLUSION

In summary, the three main qualifications to keep in mind when seeking to identify up-and-coming evangelists are: A calling from God to a specific evangelistic ministry that has been confirmed by the local church, and obvious possession of the skills necessary to carry out the ministry.

Churches beware! The prayers of past generations are resulting in a tidal wave of young evangelists! They want to talk about their ministry, and we need to know how to answer them. If you are interested in going deeper into the subject in order to be better prepared to help future evangelists, I recommend *The Power of Mentoring: Shaping People Who Will Shape the World* by Martin Sanders.[8]

---

[8]Martin Sanders, *The Power of Mentoring: Shaping People Who Will Shape the World* (Camp Hill: Christian Publications, 2004)

DIGGING DEEPER

Interview with **Lindsay Brown,** *International Director of the Lausanne Movement, evangelist with InterVarsity and founder of the FEUER program (Evangelizing college campuses in Europe)*

How would you answer a student who says to you "Lindsay, God is calling me to be an evangelist"?

I would tell him everything, the good, the bad and the ugly. I'd say, "That's wonderful! We need more evangelists in the church... there are too few. However, I'd suggest that you put your gifts to the test, in the following ways:

- Take advantage of every possible opportunity to serve, especially where you might have an opportunity to share the Gospel. Try out your gift during these occasions: Open air meetings, small groups, youth group meetings, church activities or college ministries;
- Observe how God uses you in these situations. Do people come to Christ? The mark of an evangelist is not only being able to clearly speak of God's love, but also seeing his blessing on your ministry which allows people to pass from death to eternal life;
- Ask for the opinions of people in your church who you respect such as family members and Christian friends. Invite them to critique the contents and style of your

message and to give you honest feedback about how they feel God has gifted you;

- Take the time you need to develop and sharpen your gift. Read messages written by the great evangelists, whether they be contemporary or from centuries past.
- No matter what God's call is for you specifically, seek to remain a student your whole life. Remember, there are many different types of evangelists. Some are gifted in one-on-one ministry; others are called to proclaim the Gospel publicly. These are two different kinds. Learn to discern where God is calling you.

What should I do if a parachurch organization like InterVarsity recognizes my calling as an evangelist, but my local church does not? Is that enough?

It seems to me that, according to the biblical model, gifts are recognized, appreciated, developed and confirmed in the context of the local church.

Be sure that the leaders of your local church are submitting themselves to the authority of God's Word and that they recognize the lordship and uniqueness of Jesus Christ. If this isn't the case, chances are they won't recognize the urgency of evangelism.

Otherwise, submit yourself to the church leadership – cultivating a teachable attitude and a heart that is willing to serve in the smallest tasks. God often opens bigger doors of opportunity when we assume an attitude of humility.

It's great if your university group sees your giftedness, but in my opinion, it's even more important that you have the confirmation, encouragement and blessing of your local church.

If at first your gifts are not recognized, seek to serve humbly and trust God. He will work in the hearts of your church leaders who will one day identify and confirm your gifting.

Can I call myself an evangelist even if I've never had the privilege of leading someone to Christ?

In the New Testament, Paul says that some people sow, others teach and others reap the harvest.

One of the principal characteristics of an evangelist is that he or she is capable of helping someone take the step of faith which is necessary in order to pass from death to eternal life. In my opinion, one of the marks of an evangelist is seeing people put their trust in Christ as a result of his message.

On the other hand, some of us are working in extremely hostile cultures, and we must patiently wait for God's working in the midst of materialism, hedonism and secularism.

It may just be that you need to be patient a while longer and trust God to bring your ministry to fruition.

What, in your opinion, are the main types of evangelists in the context of university campuses?

We see a need for all kinds of evangelists: artists, apologists, preachers, etc. The church needs people who have a passion for what the apostle calls "persuasive evangelism" (cf. Acts 17). The ability to communicate the truth, the power and the wonder of the Gospel are desperately needed in Europe, especially in the French-speaking world. We need people who can preach the Gospel to a large audience.

I don't believe that the New Testament separates apologetics from evangelism. The kind of evangelism we see most often in the book of Acts is persuasive or rational evangelism.

This style of evangelism brings forth the truth of the Gospel as well as its timeless appeal.

In the first few verses of Acts 8, we see two different types of evangelism at work among the believers in the church of Antioch. Some of them have a gift for publicly proclaiming the Gospel, while others are gifted at sharing on a personal level. We need both of these styles on university campuses, and in the world as a whole, as well as people who pray faithfully and live lives wholly consecrated to God.

There are several primary needs, even though, of course, the main idea is to share the Gospel with as many people as possible, by any means possible. This includes visual and artistic mediums. In my opinion, theater, music and other art forms are extremely useful, as long as they serve the spoken Word.

We must work seriously and consider how to accurately communicate a message which is essentially based on words (Jesus is the Word, our message is found in the words of Scripture, we use words to communicate with others) in a world which is more and more saturated with visual images. As a whole, the evangelical world has not succeeded in thinking seriously about this subject.

CHAPTER 3

DOWN WITH CRIMINALS!

The evangelist's personal life

Ein Evangelist ohne Charakter ist ein Krimineller![1]
[An evangelist devoid of character is a criminal!]

I can still hear Ulrich Parzany speak these words. We were traveling through Germany with a group of young evangelists to meet with several influential men in the field of evangelism. I saw the young people nodding their heads in agreement as he spoke the words. *Ein Krimineller.* No more and no less. Am I *ein Krimineller*?

THE EVANGELIST MUST LIVE A HOLY LIFE

In his first epistle, Peter strongly reminds us to:

"... honor Christ the Lord as holy [in your hearts], always being prepared to make a defense to anyone who asks you for a reason for the hope that is in you; yet do it with gentleness

[1]Words from Ulrich Parzany, "Jesus House" meeting in Stuttgart, 2011.

and respect, having a good conscience, so that, when you are slandered, those who revile your good behavior in Christ may be put to shame. For it is better to suffer for doing good, if that should be God's will, than for doing evil" (1 Peter 3:15-17).

The proclamation of the Gospel cannot be dissociated from a holy life. We must sanctify (*hagiasate*) the Lord Jesus Christ in our hearts as holy, always keeping in mind the hope that is in us. This is true for every Christian, particularly for the evangelist whose message must be reflected in his life.

This was Billy Graham's battle cry. He talks about it in his autobiography:

> From time to time, Cliff, Bev, Grady, and I talked among ourselves about the recurring problems many evangelists seemed to have, and about the poor image so-called mass evangelism had in the eyes of many people. Sinclair Lewis's fictional character Elmer Gantry unquestionably had given traveling evangelists a bad name. To our sorrow, we knew that some evangelists were not much better than Lewis's scornful caricature.[2]

In order to protect the message of the Gospel, Billy Graham set up a series of resolutions to help him maintain the biblical standards of purity that all evangelists must aspire to. Knowing that Ulrich Parzany's ministry in Germany is a result of Billy Graham's influence in his life, it's easy to understand why personal integrity is so important to him.

The Bible speaks often about personal integrity. Let's look at some biblical definitions to get warmed up.

---

[2]Billy Graham, *Just As I Am: The Autobiography of Billy Graham* (New York: Guideposts, 1997), 127.

Kittel reminds us that the Greek verb *hagiazô* is only found in the New Testament, and that it means to consecrate or sanctify.[3] We are called to sanctify Christ in our hearts, living irreproachable lives because Christ has called us out and he sanctifies us by his presence in our hearts: "You shall be holy, for I am holy" (1 Peter 1:16). That's the final word. But how do we live out this holiness on a daily basis?

Amy Orr-Ewing, evangelist and Director of Programs for the Oxford Centre for Christian Apologetics (the OCCA) gives us some solid clues. For Orr-Ewing, two other words in the New Testament give us a deeper understanding of what God expects of us: *proskyneô* and *latreuô.* [4]

Proskyneô implies falling at Jesus' feet because He is the King. Like the wise men who travelled from the East to bow down before the holy child (Matthew 2:11), or the disciples who fell prostrate before their Master when he calmed the storm.

When we fall down before Jesus Christ, nothing else matters. We lay our lives down at his feet. All of our projects, our plans for the future, our ambitions, our wildest dreams, everything fades away before His majesty.

The apostle John reminds us that God is spirit and that "those who worship Him must worship in spirit and truth" (John 4:24). I cannot worship Jesus if I'm holding back on even one little corner of my life – if I'm saying to myself, "I'll

[3]Gerhard Kittel, *Theological Dictionary of the New Testament* (Grand Rapids: Eerdmans, 1995)
[4]Amy Orr-Ewing, "Introduction to Spiritual Disciplines," in *Vital Connections* (Oxford: RZIM, 2007)

just keep a little bit of my will in case things don't work out as planned." No, when I bow down before Jesus, my whole life is His.

Latreuô carries with it the general idea of good conduct translated into action. He gives us salvation so that we "might serve him without fear, in holiness and righteousness before him all our days," (Luke 1:74-75) like the widow who, at 84 years of age, "never left the temple, serving night and day with fastings and prayers" (Luke 2:37, NASB). Like Paul the evangelist who served God "in the gospel of his Son" (Romans 1:9). When we worship God, we serve him.

My grandfather was from a Mennonite background. He was a hard worker. There was a plaque on his kitchen wall with his motto written on it: PRAY AND WORK. This is what it means to serve the God who created us twice. First when He created us in Adam and then when He recreated us in Jesus Christ, the second Adam. The verb *latreuô* gives the idea of being fully committed to the work of service that God has created for us beforehand (Ephesians 2:10) and refuses the idea of separating Sunday morning from Monday morning; the sacred from the secular. It reminds us that our daily work is also a part of our call, as Calvin said.

When our lives are totally submitted to God (*proskyneô*) and totally dedicated to his service (*latreuô*), then we know that we are living a consecrated life, one where Christ is set apart (*hagiazô*) in our hearts. This is the first prerequisite for biblical evangelism. Jesus taught it. Paul shows us how to do it. Peter reminds us of it. We would be fools to ignore it. Down with criminals!

TEN CHARACTER TRAITS WE NEED TO DEVELOP

One key to getting rid of criminals is a good dose of prevention.

If we want our "evangelistic streets" to be safe places once again, we need to warn young evangelists, train them, encourage them and reprimand them when necessary. We find ten principal character traits which need to be developed in the life of anyone who aspires to this wonderful ministry.

1. Living a life which is set apart

We talked a little bit about this earlier in the chapter. In the appendix you'll find a questionnaire compiled by Dr. Bill Jones, president of Columbia International University, called "Without Blame." It's really quite simple. For every character trait that Jesus emphasizes in the Sermon on the Mount, you'll find three questions to help you make sure that you are still on course. Beware of self-deceit! As you complete the exercise, the Holy Spirit will make it clear to you if there are areas where you may be sinning. Beware of hypocrisy; if the Spirit convicts you of sin, confess it! Confessing simply means saying out loud what God has already seen in secret.

An evangelist makes David's prayer his own: "Behold, you delight in truth in the inward being, and you teach me wisdom in the secret heart" (Psalm 51:6), and takes Paul's injunction to heart when he says, "Walk in wisdom toward outsiders, making the best use of the time" (Colossians 4:5).

Let's be wise evangelists who live out the truth in our inward being. Living a life of wisdom means putting into practice the little I actually know. It means resisting the temptation to rationalize my sin: "Yeah I know I have a problem in that area, but I make up for it in other areas!" How sad. Not only is the evangelist called to live a life which is set apart, but Paul reminds us that it should show on the outside. In other words, my coworkers, my parents, my wife or husband and my children should all be able to evaluate the degree of sanctification in my life! Does that scare you? It should. Down with criminals!

Lord, teach me to live a life which is set apart.

2. Depending on the power of the Holy Spirit

The evangelist must not only be filled with the Spirit and walk therein, he must also place all of his trust in the power of the Holy Spirit. This is a trap for so many of us who, after getting a few miles under our belts in the ministry, may be tempted to forget to lean on the Spirit's power. This is what we call serving in the flesh. The sad thing is that it often works, at least for a while. It is possible to bear fruit, even to see people saved, in the power of our flesh. Evangelism becomes merely a technique. The same messages are preached every time, and they are tweaked to perfection. We know how to manipulate an audience, what touches their hearts, what makes them cry. We are masters in the art of the Gospel invitation. We tell ourselves that we are doing a good job, that the Lord must certainly be pleased with us. But deep down inside, we are filled with sorrow. Our hearts are divided between who we seem to be and who we really are. Think about it! How long has this been going on? Ever since we started trying to take the glory for ourselves. Ever since the portrait of our ministry started to show us alone at the center. Alone. That's the word for it. "And do not grieve the Holy Spirit of God, by whom you were sealed for the day of redemption" (Ephesians 4:30). Down with criminals!

3. Learning to pray

Edward Bounds wrote more on this subject than anyone else. That's probably because it mirrored his personal life experience. In his eight-volume authoritative work on the subject, he covers the necessity of prayer, the essentials of prayer, the possibilities, reality and results of prayer, the weapon of prayer, the power of prayer and finally, men of prayer. A written monument to a monumental subject! He wrote:

> There may be much bowing of the head, and yet there may be no serious, real praying. Prayer is real work. Praying is vital work.[5]

We agree, we confess it, we know we should pray more. But how much more? What exactly does Paul mean when he tells the Colossians to "Continue steadfastly in prayer, being watchful in it with thanksgiving" (Colossians 4:2).

If prayer is actually hard work, vital work, then maybe we should begin by learning to pray. That's where the disciples began: "Lord, teach us to pray, as John taught his disciples" (Luke 11:1). John Ortberg says it this way, "There is an immense difference between training to do something and trying to do something. [...] Spiritual transformation is not a matter of trying harder, but of training wisely."[6] In other

---

[5]Edward Bounds, *The Complete Works of E. M. Bounds on Prayer* (Grand Rapids: Baker Books, 2000), book IV, 230.

[6]John Ortberg, *The Life You've Always Wanted* (Grand Rapids: Zondervan, 1997), 17.

words, if we want our prayers to be heard and to have an impact on the world around us, we must learn to pray better. Yes, prayer is a learned skill.

It is vital that the evangelist himself, more than any other servant of the Lord, know how to pray, and be able to teach others to pray, just as John the Baptist did with his disciples and Jesus did with his. I am part of a community of prayer and intercession. It's called a church. Early every morning, we meet for an hour for prayer punctuated by times of praise, silence, Bible reading and meditation, prayer for the persecuted Church and intercession for those around us. Every weeknight, we meet to share how and where God answered our prayers. We thank him for his faithfulness and his goodness. That's a total of seven hours of prayer per week. We have learned to persevere in prayer. It was hard in the beginning, but over time, it became a natural and expected part of our day. Yes, prayer is hard work. "Prayer must be a habit, but also... Prayer is the deep secret of a soul molded after God's image."[7] It is only then that our prayers become realistic, because they are inspired by the mind of God.

Lord, teach us to pray!

4. Recognizing God's glory in all circumstances

Evangelist Leighton Ford published a book on cultivating an attentive life.[8] When I asked him why he wrote on that specific subject, he answered, "Because I don't know how to be attentive. I'm an evangelist... full speed ahead! I had to

---

[7]Bounds, book I.

[8]Leighton Ford, *The Attentive Life: Discerning God's Presence in All Things* (Downers Grove : IVP, 2008)

learn to pay attention to the presence of God in my everyday life."

Recognizing the glory of God in all situations; that's quite an agenda!

When our church gets together every evening to share how God has answered our prayers, we each answer the following question: "Where was God today?" It's amazing how forgetful we can be. I find myself conscious of God's presence until about noon. Once lunch is over, I've already forgotten the prayer requests that were shared that morning. I forget to pay attention. I'm inattentive to God's presence, to the point that I no longer see his glory shining forth in the little things. What a shame. How can I proclaim God's glory to the world if I refuse to see it in my daily life? It's absurd!

Lord, help me to recognize your glory, in all situations!

5. Walking by faith

His name is Larry. The first time I met him, I thought he was a houseboy. He hastened to put our suitcases on the roof of the car the mission had sent for us: "Welcome to Chad! We are so happy to have you with us!" Several months later, I ran into Larry again, this time in the southern part of the country where we were living. He asked me lots of questions about why we had decided to do our civil service in Chad and about our plans for the future. He wanted to know all the details! I finally turned the conversation towards him, and asked, "And you, Larry, tell me about yourself."

He described how, after several years of research in the field of theology, he was asked to open a Bible institute for students who could barely read or write. He agreed, despite thinking that the endeavor would be akin to intellectual suicide for someone with his level of studies. He had traveled the country many times, leading workshops for pastors who were starved for biblical teaching. He came to love these men as his sons, and had even learned the local dialects so that he could better serve them.

He was quite familiar with the hospital where we were working, having lost his son to a post-operative hemorrhage after an appendectomy. I remembered having gone past his gravesite when we arrived in Chad several months before.

"My life hasn't always been easy," he said. He talked about how Sudanese Muslim fundamentalists had broken into his house, threatening to put a bullet through his cook's head in front of his wife and children who were kneeling on the floor.

But despite all of that, he loved his adoptive country, and he loved its people. His burden for lost souls and his devotion to see pastors trained was so deep that nothing could take him away from his mission field.

Larry is a man who walks by faith. I felt it in my bones as we prayed together and he begged Jesus to come back soon so that he could see His face, in all of His glory. I, on the other hand, had recently gotten married and in my heart I was praying, "Lord, not now. Give me a few more months to enjoy my wife!"

The apostle Paul said: "… we walk by faith, not by sight. Yes, we are of good courage, and we would rather be away from the body and at home with the Lord" (2 Corinthians 5:7-8). This means living in the present with an eternal perspective.

Paul concludes: "For we must all appear before the

judgment seat of Christ, so that each one may receive what is due for what he has done in the body, whether good or evil. Therefore, knowing the fear of the Lord, we persuade others. But what we are is known to God, and I hope it is known also to your conscience" (2 Corinthians 5:10-11).

Lord, make me like Larry. Teach me to walk by faith!

6. A fresh spirituality

We have all seen deodorant commercials. You know, the ones I'm talking about, where someone leaps out of the shower, joyfully applies the latest miracle roll-on, and then dances through the streets, smiling at everyone they meet. They feel fresh! All day long! Up to 48 hours of freshness, they proclaim.

Too bad we can't find a can of spiritual freshness in our local drugstore. I'd take a dozen of those right now.

Spiritual freshness is the opposite of a tired, faded spirituality. The evangelist must pay attention to his spiritual health; this also means being attentive to the state of his physical and emotional health.

When we are physically exhausted, we set ourselves up for an emotional roller-coaster ride, and our spiritual life suffers. On the other hand, when we are well-rested we have a much better chance of feeling good emotionally, and our spiritual energy is renewed.

I always wonder when I hear evangelists boasting about their overloaded ministry schedules. "What? Take a day off? I don't have the time for that my friend. I'm burning the candle at both ends." They're always running, going to meeting after meeting, recycling their sermons, developing symptoms of physical strain (reflux, insomnia, palpitations) until they finally break down. And that's the end of their overworked schedule.

> Six days shall work be done, but the seventh day is a Sabbath of solemn rest, holy to the Lord. Whoever does any work on the Sabbath day shall be put to death. Therefore the people of Israel shall keep the Sabbath, observing the Sabbath throughout their generations, as a covenant forever. It is a sign forever between me and the people of Israel that in six days the Lord made heaven and earth, and on the seventh day he rested and was refreshed (Exodus 31:15-17).

Cultivating one's spiritual freshness begins by learning how to rest. It's one of the Ten Commandments. If God put it in His commandments, it must be important. The Sabbath principle runs throughout history. God established it in the book of Genesis before the fall; it is a part of his creational structure. He reminds us that the world is awaiting its redemption, according to Hebrews 4:9-11, therefore making it an eschatological symbol. The Sabbath reminds us where we came from and where we are going.

On the Sabbath, God restores all that we have given out on the other six days. The seventh day, we learn to cease from work, so that God can work in us. He restores us physically, emotionally and spiritually. If I refuse to take a day off, it's as if I were saying to God, "I don't need you to restore me; I still have a little bit to give."

We can also refresh ourselves outside of the Sabbath day, through reading, hobbies, spiritual disciplines, getting together with friends or traveling. All of these things feed our souls, and are crucial to the healthy evangelist.

Lord, teach me to cultivate a fresh spirituality!

7. A healthy family life

Evangelists are often a bad example in this area. Yes, spiritual battles are a reality. Yes, travel is a part of your ministry if you are an itinerant evangelist. Yes, our children are free to make their own decisions in life. But, let's be honest, we have a lot of progress to make in the area of family relationships.

Every time I see Edward, he asks me the same question: "When's the last time you spent time with your wife and kids?" Every time! Edward makes sure that I'm taking care of my family. Recently, Martin Sanders, who mentors countless evangelists, stayed at our house. He later confessed to me why he wanted to stay with us: "I wanted to see how your family was really doing. I'm reassured."

A good evangelist knows that the people who most need to see his testimony are the members of his own family. It's so obvious, yet seems so complicated.

I have heard people say things like, "No one is a prophet in his own country," or "God will raise someone up to take care of my children as long as I'm taking care of His."

It's amazing how easy it is for criminals to justify themselves!

Here are some simple rules that I learned from my mentor Roy King that may help you in this area:

1. Be sure that at least four evenings out of seven are set aside exclusively for family during the first years of your

ministry. If you invite someone over to your house, that evening doesn't count!

2. If you need to be away for ministry, take the day off before you leave in order to get ready for the trip. Take off at least a half-day after you get back as well.
3. Happy wife, happy life! If you see that your wife is unhappy, stop everything and find out why!
4. Children grow up so fast. If your ministry takes you away from home often, be intentional in creating memories with them. Take fun vacations; celebrate important birthdays (i.e. their tenth or their eighteenth) in a memorable fashion.
5. To avoid your family developing an allergy to the ministry, try to mix fun and service whenever you can. For example, take your family skiing when you're invited to speak in the mountains.

The list could go on and on, but you get the idea. Lord, help me to watch over my family!

8. Sharing your spiritual journey on a regular basis

It might seem strange to see this characteristic included in the list. But you'd be surprised how easy it is for an evangelist to become "professional," thus forgetting to share his own personal testimony with those who God brings across his path.

I've heard so many complaints from those who organize evangelistic campaigns about speakers who are rude to the very volunteers who have given their time so that the evening can run smoothly.

Another trap evangelists often fall into is teaching without actually putting what they say into practice. For example:

"If you want to be an effective evangelist, you just need to put my five basic principles into practice. 1, 2, 3, 4, 5! Got it?"

"Ok, but how do you live those principles out practically?"

"Umm... Next question please?"

One thing that has really helped me in this area is to keep one foot in the church-planting world. This keeps me at the heart of one-on-one evangelism. Church planting allows you to practice what you preach and to make sure it really works. It's amazing, the best of both worlds! Whether you are involved in church planting or not, you must be sure to regularly share your personal testimony. Otherwise you may be disqualified from the ministry as you teach people one thing, but live another.

Lord, I want to share my testimony often!

9. A true compassion for the poor

When Paul traveled to Jerusalem to meet with the apostles where they would confer upon him his mission to the Gentiles, they reminded him to remember the poor: "the very thing I was eager to do," he said (Galatians 2:10).

Paul had already proven his burden for the needy on his earlier trip to Jerusalem in Acts 11:27-30. He was encouraged to persevere in his compassion during the Council. This motivated Paul to press on in collecting offerings from the churches in Asia Minor and in Europe which would be destined for the poor in Judea who were suffering from several famines, as well as at the hands of their Roman oppressors

(Acts 24:17; Romans 15:26; 1 Corinthians 16:3-4; 2 Corinthians 8-9).

One of my co-workers, Saotra, lives in a hostel for young workers. It's not because he can't afford to live anywhere else but because he has chosen to live there. It is a way for him to remember those who have less than he does. I am fascinated and encouraged by his generosity. What a powerful life testimony!

Let's remember what the Cape Town Commitment[9] says:

> Above all we must replace self-interest and greed with the biblical teaching on self-sacrifice and generous giving as the marks of true discipleship to Christ. We affirm Lausanne's historic call for simpler lifestyles.
>
> *Cape Town Commitment, II.E.A*

Lord, fill me with compassion for those less fortunate than I am!

10. Remember the big picture

The evangelist is concerned with the salvation of those around him, in his neighborhood, his city, his state, and his country. But he can become shortsighted, confusing his mission field with that of the entire world.

In Matthew 28:19, Jesus says, "Go therefore and make disciples of all nations." The mission field includes all nations,

---

[9]The Third Lausanne Congress on World Evangelization (Cape Town, 16-25 October 2010) brought together 4,200 evangelical leaders from 198 countries to bring a fresh challenge to the global Church to bear witness to Jesus Christ and all his teaching - in every nation, in every sphere of society, and in the realm of ideas. The Cape Town Commitment is the fruit of this endeavor. It stands in an historic line, building on both The Lausanne Covenant and The Manila Manifesto.

all ethnic groups, those who live in our country as well as those who live outside of our borders.[10]

One-third of all people cannot know Jesus as their Savior, because no one around them can tell them about him.

Does my country need the Gospel? Absolutely, but my country is not "all nations." There is so much to be done in the world at large. Think about North Africa for example, or the Comoro Islands. The situation is tragic in these areas. Evangelists must go forth to speak with those who have not yet received the Gospel. Jesus commands us to do so; he commands us to make disciples of all nations!

My friend Jason, from Operation World, likes to remind people that a nation's spiritual vitality seems to be directly linked to its propensity to bless other nations through evangelism. Here is a list of the countries that send the highest number of evangelists to other unreached nations, proportional to the number of Christians in their country.

1. Mongolia	1:222
2. Lebanon	1:295
3. Singapore	1:400
4. Nigeria	1:451
5. Nepal	1:458
6. Sri Lanka	1:479
7. Spain	1:512
8. Faroe Islands	1:533
9. Mali	1:608
10. Thailand	1:633

[10]For more information about non-evangelized areas, visit Joshua Project website: http://www.JoshuaProject.net (last consulted on September 2, 2013)

Think on that for a while.

If we want God to bless our country, we need to take Mongolia as our example!

Having a vision for the nations also means that we obtain a new understanding of our current prosperity theology and that we embrace a theology of suffering. As Neil Cole said during the 2010 Evangelist's Forum in Lyon:

> In order for the seed to fall into the earth and bear fruit, it must die. We have a prosperity theology, but do we have a theology of death to self?[11]

We have much to learn from our colleagues who risk their very lives in order to stay committed to the greater mission.

Lord, forgive me; I want to stay committed to the big picture!

IN CONCLUSION

That was a long list! Ten character traits which are essential in the personal life of the evangelist, we have some work ahead of us!

When we interviewed the majority of the young evangelists coming out of our R2E program, it was interesting to observe three results which came from the time they spent with us:

- The training program allowed them to see significant developments in the acquisition of these character traits
- Once the program was completed, the evangelists felt that

[11]Neil Cole, The Evangelist Forum, 2010

they had acquired these traits and were continuing to work on them

- Those who saw the most fruit in their personal ministry were the ones who had successfully acquired all of the character traits, especially walking by faith and a deep prayer life. Aren't those the two things that the disciples asked their Master to work into their lives as well?

Conclusion? It is possible to develop these character traits. I would even go so far as to say that it is vital to our ministry. "An evangelist devoid of character is a criminal!"

DIGGING DEEPER

Interview with **Alain Stamp***, Evangelist, author and mentor with France Evangelization*

How do you maintain freshness in your spiritual life after so many years of serving as an evangelist?

I think it's so important to maintain an attitude of wonder in our Christian life and in our service; being constantly amazed by God, His love, His grace, His Word and His works.

Sometimes people ask me how I stay so energetic, and I tell them (and I'm not kidding): "It's not hard! Look at what God is doing in the world and particularly in the lives of the new generation of leaders that I have the privilege of accompanying! That's enough to keep anyone enthused!"

Another important aspect is the capacity to repent… quickly! Getting older doesn't necessarily mean that we are becoming better Christians. But it's so refreshing to know that we can plead guilty as soon as – and as often as – we need to! To be immediately restored in our relationship with Christ and not remain separated from him. We don't need to be stressed about defending ourselves or about repairing what we've damaged. We only have to recognize our wrongs, plead guilty and change our attitude toward them. We are instantly forgiven, purified by God and restored in our relationships with others. We waste so much energy trying to pretend that all is well, while that still, small voice of the Spirit is inviting us to acknowledge our need for God's grace. In our couples, in our work relationships, being able to take responsibility for our sins is so liberating, so refreshing. That's what it means to live life connected to the source.

Of course, just like anyone else, I need to be careful to be disciplined in my reading, prayer life and Bible study if I want to stay fresh! We can never take these things for granted.

Evangelists are often called to work alone in the mission field. Should an evangelist be accountable for his personal life? If so, to whom?

I had the privilege of being introduced to the ministry by a brother who was, and still is today, my mentor. We're kind of like Paul and Timothy. I don't believe anyone can remain in the ministry for long playing the Lone Ranger, without being followed up by someone who serves as a mentor in his life. Every evangelist, every servant of God, needs encouragement, exhortation and sometimes, even correction. He needs to be able to share his fears, his dreams and his disappointments, to seek help managing his successes as well as his failures... to open his heart, to share his doubts... all this without any fear of being judged or evaluated! He needs someone to whom he can ask the right questions. How can we expect an evangelist to keep on the right path with the right attitude, not to take up some crazy project without the advice of a more mature brother who listens and who burns with passion for his ministry?

So, the answer is yes, every evangelist should have a mentor who has the right to examine his life, to whom he is accountable and who can accompany him in his character development. This can vary from one mentoring relationship to the other, but the goal is always the same: to offer a friendship which also ensures a degree of discipleship and spiritual support.

Is fear a normal part of the ministry of an evangelist?

Fear is a normal part of life. In the ministry, we face the fear of not being good enough, of making mistakes and bad choices, of being criticized, of not being well-prepared and so many other things. For those who are in full time ministry, there is also the fear of financial struggles. I remember back when I was a young evangelist/church planter, just after my daughter was born, feeling panicked and thinking, "Will I be able to provide this little girl with any kind of future?" I really had to throw myself into God's arms for that panic to subside. And he has always provided for all of our needs since that day.

Some fears are the result of emotional difficulties. A good mentor can be very helpful in these situations to help the person regain confidence in him or herself.

Other fears provide us with an excellent opportunity to put all of our trust in God. In these situations, fear is a good thing. One day, back when I was doing a lot of evangelism through song with a group of amazing musicians, a young man came up to me, full of admiration and enthusiasm and said, "I'd like to be like you one day and be up there on the stage."

I answered him, "I never get up here without my knees shaking, without putting everything that I am, my thoughts, what others might say or think about me (the folly of the Gospel) on the altar, into God's hands. And every time, I have to die to myself a little bit more!"

What would you say to an evangelist who is suffering and believes that God is taking his ministry away from him?

Wow, that's a big question, and not an easy one! But it's essential to keep this in mind when you are going through trials. It was God who called you and it was God who entrusted you with your ministry. Your gifts are simply a result of his generosity. Therefore, only he can take these things away from you, no one else. Not your circumstances or your trials or your suffering, whatever they may be. Whether your situation is favorable or seemingly impossible, everything depends on God Himself. When my first wife became ill and we knew she wouldn't be coming out of the hospital, I went through some times of real despair. One day, I said to my mentor, "This is too hard for me. I'm at the end of my rope, it's all too much. I'm going to step out of the ministry."

His answer was simply, "If you think you can stop, then go ahead."

And I couldn't. God didn't let me stop. Not because I was any better than anyone else, but because God was watching over me, over my call and over my ministry. He was the Master over my situation. Don't let your trials rob you of what God has entrusted to you.

However, there is one thing that can disqualify you in the ministry, and that is sin. It is often when we are in the midst of trials and suffering, and therefore weak, that we are the most tempted. So, when we are going through hard times, we need to be twice as careful. We need to put into practice the advice that Paul gave to Timothy: "... be strengthened by the grace that is in Christ Jesus" (2 Timothy 2:1).

CHAPTER 4

TALKING ABOUT GOD ISN'T A JOB

The ministry of the evangelist

"Daddy, what do you do for a living?"
"I'm an evangelist."
"No, I mean what's your *real* job?"
"I'm really an evangelist."
"But talking about God isn't a job!"
Some conversations are harder to swallow than others.

THE EVANGELIST: GIFT OF GAB OR ASSISTANT PASTOR?

What do evangelists really do with their time? That's a good question! Some people, like my son, think they spend all day talking to others about God, from morning to night. We are all called to talk to others about God, to give a reason for the hope that is in us (1 Peter 3:15). Our words must be sprinkled with a sort of divine vinaigrette and be "gracious, seasoned with salt" (Colossians 4:6). Evangelists are asked to be an example of this. But this is not their only responsibility… there is more!

For others, an evangelist is a wannabe pastor or an "almost-but-not-quite" pastor because there is just something missing: Formal theological training, the gift of leadership or whatever it might be. For some, the position of evangelist is the booby prize for those who play the pastoral lottery. We entrust them with the second-rate jobs, hoping they will be content to fulfill their responsibilities with a good attitude. Normally they do, all the while wondering if there shouldn't be something else to their ministry.

In some circles, we even go so far as to define the ministry of the evangelist in relation to that of the pastor: "You are a pastor evangelist." In other words, you fulfill all of the responsibilities of a pastor, plus those of an evangelist. Everyone's happy, it's the best of both worlds and people don't look at you quite so strangely when you talk to them in the street:

"So, what do you do?"

"I'm an evangelist."

"A what?"

"A pastor."

"Oh, ok, well, that's interesting."

We have gotten away from a biblical definition of the evangelist. We need to redefine our concept of the ministry of evangelist, not only in the light of tradition, but especially in the light of the Scriptures.

SIX RESPONSIBILITIES OF AN EVANGELIST[1]

An evangelist ministers in the church and outside of it. He navigates between the two. Outside the church, his goal is to see the lost reached for Christ. Inside the church, he trains Christians how to practice evangelism themselves. Philip the evangelist (Acts 21:8) is our model for this ministry.

The evangelist's responsibilities outside the church

1. The evangelist crosses religious, social and cultural boundaries

When Philip arrives in Samaria after the great persecution of the Church led by Saul of Tarsus (Acts 8:1), he is confronted with his first hurdle. How can he reach the Samaritans who follow a different religion than his? This is the religious boundary.

The religious boundary

It is very difficult for anyone, even an evangelist, to navigate in a religious setting that is different from his own. Every religion has similarities and differences with the message of salvation. The evangelist must find the similarities and use them in conversation so as to open a door for his message, without minimizing the differences. The apostle Paul, who was responsible for Philip's being sent to Samaria, gives us an excellent example of this apologetic approach when he speaks to the Athenians in Acts 17. He finds their similarities: "Men

[1] I am indebted here to the work of Lon Allison, executive director of the Billy Graham Center at Wheaton College on the Portrait of the Evangelist.

of Athens, I perceive that in every way you are very religious" (Acts 17:22). He shares the message of the Gospel with them (God is the Creator, man seeks him, God wants to save man, man must repent) and emphasizes their differences (divine judgment and the resurrection of the dead).

Here is where we need to be careful. Evangelists are often tempted to err either on the side of syncretism (minimizing the differences: "It's true, when you get right down to it, we all believe in the same God") or on the side of arrogance (minimizing the similarities: "These people can't teach me anything!")

The Cape Town Commitment says it well:

> We affirm the proper place for dialogue with people of other faiths, just as Paul engaged in debate with Jews and Gentiles in the synagogue and public arenas. As a legitimate part of our Christian mission, such dialogue combines confidence in the uniqueness of Christ and in the truth of the gospel with respectful listening to others.
>
> *Cape Town Commitment, II.C.1.e*

The social boundary

After leaving Samaria, Philip took the Gaza road to Jerusalem, under orders from an angel of the Lord:

> And there was an Ethiopian, a eunuch, a court official of Candace, queen of the Ethiopians, who was in charge of all her treasure. He had come to Jerusalem to worship and was returning, seated in his chariot, and he was reading the prophet Isaiah. And the Spirit said to Philip, "Go over and join this chariot." So Philip ran to him and heard him reading Isaiah the prophet and asked, "Do you understand what you are reading?" (Acts 8:27-30).

I love this passage. It reminds us of Philip's total dependence on the Holy Spirit (Chapter 3). Running after a chariot doesn't necessarily fall under the responsibilities of the evangelist, but then again, why not? It might not be a bad idea to keep him on his toes both physically and spiritually!

Now Philip had to confront another hurdle, the social boundary. Not only was the person he was chasing from another culture (Ethiopian) and another social level (the equivalent of the Secretary of the Treasury in the American government), he might as well have been from another universe (he was a eunuch). Jewish law forbade eunuchs from taking part in the assembly of the Lord (Deuteronomy 23:1), which meant that even though he worshiped God, he could never assume the position of a proselyte (Isaiah 56:3-5). It's not surprising that the eunuch identified with the Suffering Servant of Isaiah 53 – elect, yet rejected!

Philip preached the message of Jesus Christ, who, more than any other prophet identified with those who were on the fringes of society. Jesus the evangelist crossed over all the social boundaries and Philip followed in His footsteps.

"Do you understand what you are reading?"

"How can I, unless someone guides me?"

And he invited Philip to come up and sit with him (Acts 8:30-31).

In one of the churches in the city of Grenoble, France, some of the members of the youth group get up two hours earlier on Sunday to go share God's love with the homeless. They cross social boundaries and sit with these people to lead them to the One who is the truth and the life. When they get to church, they apologize for smelling like street people and hesitate to shake your hand. But they are the ones who carry the odor of Christ, dead and risen for the world!

The cultural boundary

Once Philip had baptized the eunuch, the Spirit carried him away, and he found himself in Azotus: "and as he passed through he preached the gospel to all the towns until he came to Caesarea" (Acts 8:40). It is likely that Philip was from a Hellenistic background. In Greek, his name means "he who loves horses, a warrior." He spent his first years of ministry in the Jerusalem church, where the Greek and Jewish cultures coexisted politely for the most part, although they clashed on occasion. Philip was chosen by the apostles because of his wisdom and his good reputation in the church (Acts 6:3). He knew how to navigate the stormy waters of cultural differences.

But let's catch up with Philip. He's come to Caesarea hoping to plant a church there. The town founded by Herod the Great and named for Caesar Augustus, was the Roman capital of the province of Judah for over 600 years. Caesarea also served as the headquarters for the Roman legions stationed there. Romans, Syrians, Greeks and Jews lived there, and we can only imagine the cultural tension between these communities. This rugged location was the perfect setting for our all-terrain evangelist!

Philip was a transcultural evangelist who preached a transcultural message. It is fascinating to watch the spread of Christianity worldwide, in every culture, and to see how the different people groups embraced it while retaining their own specific cultural expression. The 3rd International Congress on World Evangelization in Cape Town was an excellent example of this cultural diversity, with over 4,500 representatives of the evangelical church from around the world! I remember listening to a group of female evangelists from India, draped in their multicolored saris. These women have a powerful ministry among street children while heading up a flourishing business. Can you imagine this happening in your country? Talk about culture shock!

> We love the world of nations and cultures. 'From one man, God made all nations of humanity, to live on the whole face of the earth.' Ethnic diversity is the gift of God in creation and will be preserved in the new creation, when it will be liberated from our fallen divisions and rivalry. Our love for all peoples reflects God's promise to bless all nations on earth and God's mission to create for Himself a people drawn from every tribe, language, nation and people.
>
> *Cape Town Commitment*, I.7.b

The evangelist's number one task is to meet with those who are outside the Church. In order to do this, he must be ready to cross over religious, social and cultural boundaries. Gernot Elsner, founder of Gospel Tribe, organizes a yearly summer camp for our young evangelists called Mission Extreme. If you like challenging experiences and goose bumps, this camp is the one for you! Our young people head out for ten days without knowing where they are going – or how they'll get back. They learn to cross religious boundaries as they share their faith with Muslims in North Africa, social boundaries as they spend twenty-four hours in the red-light district of Amsterdam and cultural boundaries as they clean up a flooded farm in southern Poland. They follow Gernot, they watch him and they imitate him. Gernot is a modern-day Philip!

2. The evangelist proclaims the Gospel.

"Now those who were scattered went about preaching [*euangelizomenoi*] the Word. Philip went down to the city of Samaria and proclaimed [*ekeryssen*] to them the Christ" (Acts 8:4-5). That is the heart of evangelism!

> When we talk about evangelism, we generally find one of three Greek words in the Bible: *euangelizô* (to announce good news), *kerussô* (to proclaim) or *martureô* (to give a testimony). *Euangelizô* is always accompanied by a direct object which describes the object of the good news (the kingdom of God, Acts 8:12; Jesus, Acts 5:42; 8:35; 17:18), whereas *kerussô* enlightens us as to the method. The message is proclaimed by a *kerux* (messenger) to those who are outside the fold of the Church. *Martureô* emphasizes the truth of the message proclaimed, as well as the credibility of the person proclaiming it.[2]

As William Temple says:

> To evangelize is to present Jesus Christ in the power of the Holy Spirit, that men shall come to put their trust in God through him, to accept him as their Savior, and serve him as their King in the fellowship of his church.[3]

[2]Raphaël Anzenberger, "Evangélisation (historique et pratique)," in *Dictionnaire de Théologie pratique*, 324.
[3]Cited by Michael Green, *Evangelism through the Local Church* (London: Hooder & Stoughton, 1990), 9.

3. The evangelist gives an invitation

Bill Jones, my evangelism professor at Columbia International University (CIU), used to tell us, "If you haven't given an opportunity for the seeker to respond, then you haven't fully evangelized!" I remember thinking to myself, "It is hard enough just to get through the Gospel presentation. If I have to invite the person to make a decision on top of everything else, I'm not sure I can do it!" I told myself that might work in America, but never in France. Oh, the exception of the French culture… so practical when I need to defend myself!

One evening while I was a student at CIU, I invited a group of fellow students for a good old American barbecue at my house with some of my coworkers from Michelin. On one side you had the dyed-in-the-wool evangelists trained by Bill Jones; on the other a bunch of purebred Frenchies "trained" by Voltaire. A little later in the evening I noticed that my evangelist friends were nowhere to be found. Had they thrown in the towel after spending time with my French friends? No way!

Chris came up to me with a big smile.

"Where were you?" I asked him.

"Oh, I took Laurent aside to talk to him about the Gospel."

"Oh, really? Was he interested?" (Surprise number one.)

"Yeah, he really listened to what I had to say. When we were done talking I asked him if he wanted to give his life to Jesus."

"So, what did he say?" (I was boiling on the inside: He's ruining everything! I have to go to work with this guy on Monday! I'm the one who will have to deal with the aftermath! This is NOT cool!)

"He said he was really interested, but he wants a little

more time before he really makes a decision. I encouraged him to talk to you about it. It was really fun!"

"Um, fun, yeah, that's a good word for it..." (Surprise number two.)

As my professor said, if you haven't given the person a chance to respond to the Gospel message, then you haven't evangelized! As it is stated in the Lausanne Covenant: "... evangelism itself is the proclamation of the historical, biblical Christ as Savior and Lord, with a view to persuading people to come to him personally and so be reconciled to God" (Article 4). To summarize, evangelism is a dual motion. The evangelist moves toward his public (proclamation), the public moves toward the evangelist and finally, toward God himself (invitation); it's a double movement from the inside to the outside, and the outside toward the inside.

When the evangelist gives an invitation, he is inviting the person to take another step toward Jesus. Each step toward Jesus is a step away from his old life. We are not asking people to adhere to a philosophical position; we are asking them to entrust their life to someone. Giving your life to Jesus Christ means changing camps: From King Me to King Jesus. An invitation should be gentle yet firm. Philip asked the eunuch, "Do you understand what you are reading?" (Acts 8:30). In the same way, Chris gently asked Laurent, "What if today was the day for you to take a step of faith? Do you want to do that together?"

Evangelists have a divine gift that allows them to be clear about the content of the message, all the while keeping the emphasis on the decision that needs to be made. They often step in at the end of a process which can take years to come to fruition. They may have the privilege of harvesting the fruit of others' labor by bringing the unbeliever to faith. In a way, an evangelist is like a midwife, preparing for new life that comes from above. He is the first one to see the newborn Christian, and that is his greatest joy!

It is because of this great joy that the moment of decision is so memorable. When a sinner is convicted by the Holy Spirit, bends his knee and opens his heart to his Lord and Savior, the evangelist's heart is filled with love and peace.

4. The evangelist lives out the Word of God through acts of compassion

You would probably be surprised to hear how some missionaries tear each other apart over this point. They say that compassion should be left to social workers, the preaching of the Gospel to evangelists. Two different calls for two different roles. Oh, really?

Philip waited tables in Acts 6. Was this a prerequisite to qualifying as an evangelist? He cast out demons and healed the sick (Acts 8:7); he also practiced hospitality when Paul and his team returned from their third missionary voyage (Acts 21:8). Philip combined acts of compassion with the proclamation of the Gospel. More than that, he actually lived out compassion in his proclamation.

In Article 5 of the Lausanne Covenant, we read:

> ... we have sometimes regarded evangelism and social concern as mutually exclusive. Although reconciliation with other people is not reconciliation with God, nor is social action evangelism, nor is political liberation

> salvation, nevertheless we affirm that evangelism and socio-political involvement are both part of our Christian duty. For both are necessary expressions of our doctrines of God and man, our love for our neighbor and our obedience to Jesus Christ.

The preaching of the Gospel must always be accompanied by acts of compassion. If I share the Gospel without proving my love by my actions, then my attitude discredits my message.

Crossing over religious, social and cultural boundaries in order to share the message of the Gospel, inviting people to respond to the message, all while living out the love of God in acts of compassion: This is the fourfold responsibility of the evangelist as he ministers to those outside the Church.

But his ministry is not limited to unbelievers. He has two other responsibilities, this time, within the Church.

The evangelist's responsibilities inside the church

5. The evangelist builds up the local church in its witness toward unbelievers

Philip didn't stop at the invitation. He went so far as to baptize the Samaritans (Acts 8:12) and the eunuch (Acts 8:38). In other words, an evangelist knows that his call doesn't stop at the moment of conversion. He needs to see the new Christian integrated into the local church through baptism. When this occurs, he can naturally hand the new believer off to someone in the church for discipleship. This should not be seen as a break in their relationship, but rather as the normal flow of events in the integration of the individual.

Evangelists can get too caught up in the outside aspect of their ministry: "Once a person is saved, he or she is the church's responsibility." Oh, really? Aren't evangelists a part of the local church? If the answer is yes, then these people are our responsibility too! We'll dig deeper into the reasons for this type of fracture in Chapter 6.

When a local church welcomes a new believer into its midst, it is a joyful occasion for everyone. The church as a whole is encouraged to continue steadfastly in prayer for those who are called to proclaim the mystery of Christ, so that God will open doors for his Word (Colossians 4:3). The evangelist receives this blessing and, in return, is a blessing to the church.

In his epistle to the Ephesians, Paul reminds us that the evangelist, along with the other functions which are described in the passage (apostle, prophet and pastor-teacher), is given to the Church "to equip [*katartismon*] the saints for the work of ministry [*diakonias*], for building up [*oikodomên*] the body of Christ" (Ephesians 4:11-12). In other words, the evangelist has a twofold ministry: equipping the saints and building up the Church.

"... To equip [*katartismon*] the saints for the work of ministry" is the responsibility of the whole community.[4] The evangelist, as a member of the local church, must do his or her part in the equipping of the saints.

In the list of different ministries found in verse 11, the evangelist has a specific role to play in the church: Training believers to share their own faith with others. The Bible tells

[4]Gerhard Kittel, *Theological Dictionary of the New Testament* (Grand Rapids: Eerdmans, 1995), 476.

us clearly that all Christians are called to give testimony to the hope that is in Christ (1 Peter 3:15; Col 4:6). It is therefore the evangelist's responsibility to develop training tools to help other Christians live a holy life which will, in turn, serve as a springboard for conversations with unbelievers. In order for this to happen, the local church must be, above all else, a praying people (cf. Chapter 3). The evangelist should serve as an example to the other members of the church.

There are numerous training tools for witnessing that can be developed in the local church. Every evangelist should be comfortable with at least one of these tools, and suggest training the members of his church either through seminars or workshops, or by actually taking other believers out on the street with him. He should also be attentive to the church's witness as a whole. How do people in the neighborhood perceive the church? How is the church perceived by the community as a whole? How can the local church be more involved locally? What are the needs, where should the church start in its efforts to serve?

Beware! There are two missiological views to steer clear of when dealing with the list of functions mentioned in Ephesians 4:11-12:

Downplaying the work of the saints

Some tend to read Ephesians 4:11-12 like this: "And he gave [...] the evangelists [...] for the work of ministry." Whew, I got rid of those pesky saints! No problem there, most church members aren't very good at evangelism anyway. I'll just take care of it myself! But, that isn't what the passage says.

Evangelism is a very powerful tool when the local church

practices it together. The Gospel that we preach is propositional (understanding the basic message, the *kerygma*) and relational (becoming part of the community of the saints). If we neglect these two aspects, we will have a very difficult time making disciples out of our new believers.

At one time, people liked to say "You believe, you belong, you behave." The hard part was going from the first point to the second one. It was almost as if we were telling people, "The good news is that you're saved. The bad news is that now you have to go to church [sic!]. I know I felt the same way."

Today, I am seeing a different way of thinking: "I belong, I behave, I believe!" In other words, the church is becoming a place where the seeker learns, discovers and imitates other believers. That's where the evangelist comes in, putting the emphasis on the need to make a personal decision.

The emergent church[5] understands this paradigm change, but has refused to embrace the theology of salvation. As a result, it has seen very little growth in numbers.

Doing away with the role of the saints

Another erroneous reading of Ephesians 4:11-12 goes something like this: "And he gave some[...] some [...] some [...] some [...] the saints [...] the body of Christ," coming to the conclusion that we are all either apostles (A), prophets (P), evangelists (E), pastors (Pa) or doctors (D). Suddenly, the saints each embody one role or another mentioned in Ephesians 4 and *voila*! Here comes the church, full steam

[5]See Brian McLaren, *Church in Emerging Culture: Five Perspectives* (Zondervan Emergent/YS, 2003)

ahead, made up only of pros. Some people go so far as to say that each Christian has a little bit of A, P, E, Pa and D in them, with at least one dominant trait. That's not what the passage says either.

If everyone is APEPaD, then why does Paul differentiate the community of the saints from these four functions in the local church? We need to be careful not to read the passage in a sociological, or even an economical, way. Missiologists dare not settle for a faulty exegesis with the excuse of being trailblazers in the area of semantics!

When these four functions (apostle, prophet, evangelist and pastor-teacher) work together in a church plant, we find what Ralph Shallis liked to call a "portable church." In other words, the APEPaD church plant team carries within itself the DNA of a new local church. Each role is carried out in symbiosis with the others and the church is built up (*oikodomên*) (Ephesians 4:12) naturally. This is the second dimension of the evangelist's role in the building up of the Body of Christ.

The evangelist must learn to work as part of a team in the local church for the growth of his ministry (Chapter 6). Philip demonstrated this as he worked in harmony with the apostles in Samaria and lived it out in his own home with his four daughters who were prophetesses.

6. The evangelist develops a vocation in others around him

The evangelist's second responsibility in the church is to develop the vocation in others.

Be careful here! It's very easy for an evangelist to concentrate all of his attention on the crowd that's following him, to the detriment of the vocations that he could be developing in the church. The success of an evangelist is often measured by the size of the crowd he gathers. What a shame!

So many "famous" evangelists have websites boasting about the number of people who come to their meetings. Woe to the evangelist who takes pride in the fruit of his ministry. We need to keep in mind all those who have labored in suffering and persecution in regions where the Gospel is met with hostility and rejection. These men and women minister without ever seeing a trace of fruit from their labors. We need to respect them and put things back into perspective. Less emphasis should be placed on the crowds who come to hear us speak and more on inspiring vocations among the saints. This is a surefire antidote for a renewed vision of ministry.

The evangelist must keep his eyes open for "young shoots." Oftentimes, God inspires a vocation in the very same people with whom we shared the Gospel not so long ago.

In our current church plant we have already identified several who have the vocation of evangelist. We identified, affirmed and trained them so that they can grow into the call that God has bestowed upon them. You would probably be surprised at how young some of them are!

Abigail, my daughter, is a good example. This book is even dedicated to her. Not long ago, her teacher called me for a parent-teacher conference. (I love you sweetheart, but this was embarrassing!)

"Do you know why I have called you to come in Mr. Anzenberger? Did Abigail tell you?"

"Um, something about passing notes in class? Rest assured, I don't approve of her doing that!"

"Yes, she has been passing notes. But did she tell you what was written on the notes?"

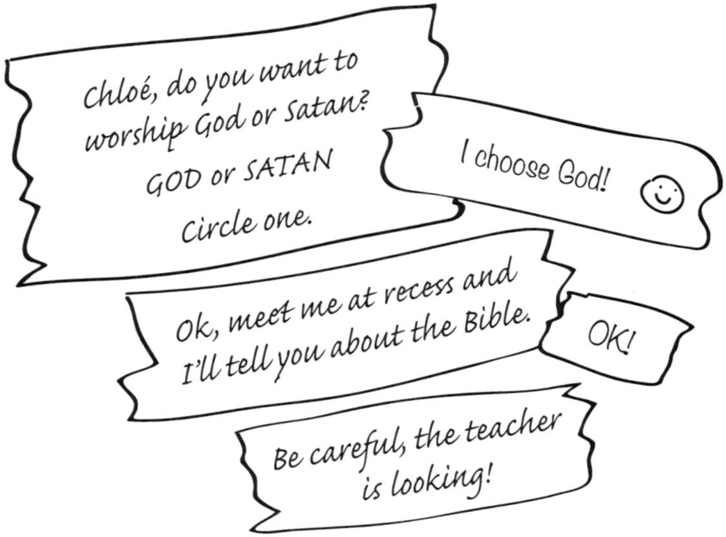

I went back to my office feeling pretty embarrassed. Rebecca and Oliver, two of our evangelists, met me at the door.

"Well, what happened?" they asked.

I showed them the notes. They were thrilled: "Go Abi! You rock!!"

What's a guy gonna do?

I feel for the apostle Philip. It must not have always been easy for him at his house. If it's not complicated enough to live with four daughters (I've only got two), just imagine four prophetesses! I'm not sure I would have survived!

IN CONCLUSION

Six responsibilities, one ministry. Crossing over religious, social and cultural boundaries; proclaiming the Gospel and inviting individuals to make a decision; being careful to live out the Word with acts of compassion; helping to equip the saints for evangelism, while overseeing the development of vocations for the ministry. The evangelist labors on both local and global levels.

The tension between the local and global ministries has always been a reality in the life of the evangelist. Philip's ministry shows us that the two dimensions don't necessarily need to be exclusive of each other. Rather, they should be combined in a healthy dynamic. The evangelist should be solidly grounded in a local church where he can fulfill his ministry to the saints (Acts 21:8; Ephesians 4:12), yet have the freedom to minister in the field to unbelievers (Acts 8). Spencer summarizes the balance that every evangelist needs to find:

> Philip's domestic-residential service in Caesarea both parallels his table waiting in Jerusalem and balances his evangelistic-itinerant mission in Judea and Samaria.[6]

[6]F. Scott Spencer, "Philip the Evangelist," in *Dictionary of the Later New Testament and its Developments* (Downers Grove: IVP, 1997), 929-931.

DIGGING DEEPER

Interview with **Saotra Rajaobelina***, evangelist, conference speaker and trainer*

How do you maintain your burden for the lost?

It's a question of relationships.

My relationship with God: God has a heart, a passion for lost souls. His love for this world is so great that he gave up what was most precious to him, his Son, to save us. As I grow in my relationship with God, I allow him to communicate his compassion for the lost to me.

My relationship with others who love God: Especially good friends of mine who are also evangelists. Every time we get together, we end up talking about evangelism, praying for people, planning projects, etc. I love the story of Peter and John in Acts 4. They had just been warned by the religious leaders of the day not to preach anymore. That couldn't have been fun for them. But, as soon as they got back to their friends their passion and enthusiasm took over once again. That day they prayed one of the most audacious prayers concerning evangelism that was ever lifted before the throne of God. I can't tell you how many times, while speaking with a fellow evangelist on the phone, our enthusiasm once again takes over, prayers are prayed and outlandish projects are conceived.

My relationship with unbelievers: You can be a professional evangelist and still never cultivate authentic friendships with non-Christians. Our passion grows as we spend time with unbelievers. We get to know them, listen to what makes them suffer, understand their worries. I lived in a college dormitory for a couple of years, and currently live in a hostel for young workers. Living with and among these young men has given me a renewed compassion for the lost.

How do you balance evangelism and social action in your ministry?

We as humans definitely feel this tension, but Jesus, who is our model, didn't seem to feel it. When Jesus preached the Gospel, it was natural for him to feed the people he was preaching to. When he healed the sick, he never hid the fact that he was on the earth for a reason.

My desire is to see all of the nations of the earth touched by the Gospel, which is why I have a particular burden for international students. Most of the young people who come to study in France have little or no Christian witness in their countries. I operate under the conviction that God has sent them here to us so that we can befriend them and share the Gospel with them.

Most of my work is done with a new organization called A Heart for the World. The group works out of an urban church in the city of Nantes. Its goal is to welcome foreign students to France. The couple who runs the ministry has made many friends with foreign students over the years. One of their friends, a young Muslim named Bakari, serves on several student committees. During Bakari's Bible studies with

Vincent, one of the missionaries, he shared numerous horror stories about other foreign students and the nightmares they have faced upon moving to France. Some have had to sleep on park benches for several nights when they arrived, because they didn't know where to go. Bakari has asked A Heart for the World to help out in these situations. They've decided that at the start of the school year next fall, they will serve as a transportation service between the airport and train stations and the campus. They have also gathered a team of believers who are willing to house students until they can find proper lodging in the city of Nantes.

Social action and evangelism go hand in hand. Far be it from me to separate the two!

What do you do to maintain close ties with your local church?

When I proclaim the Gospel, I try to remember that Jesus didn't die only for individuals, but also for his Bride, the Church. There are so many passages in the Scriptures concerning community life. If we want to live out what we preach, we must have a healthy church life. This isn't always easy for the itinerant evangelist. When I'm traveling a lot, it's easy for me to begin to feel disconnected from what's going on in my local church.

At the beginning of my ministry, the church council and I sat down and we put together some guidelines in order to facilitate my relationship with the local church. The church has recognized me as an official evangelist and I in turn have committed to preach at least once a month. I am involved in several projects with my local church, especially those having to do with missions. I also do my best to be involved in my house church group during the week. Lastly, this year, I had the privilege of discipling a young man on a weekly basis, while training others to do the same.

How do you identify future evangelists?

Identifying future evangelists is an important part of my ministry. The organization that I'm working with puts a lot of emphasis on preaching the Gospel, but also on swelling the ranks of evangelists who work with them. Because of this, whether I'm on the road preaching, or in my local church, I try to keep my eyes open for anyone I feel God may be calling to the ministry of evangelist. I'm sensitive to those who listen intently when we talk about evangelism, and whose hearts are turned toward those outside the church. Once I've discerned that someone seems to have the gift of the evangelist, I talk to them about it. It's really important for me to speak clearly with the individual, because if they really do have that gift, they have a responsibility to develop it and to mobilize the church in that direction.

Many evangelists don't know that they have the gift of the evangelist. No one has ever told them, so it's normal that their potential has never been realized. That's why, when I tell someone that I think they have the gift of evangelist, I explain the responsibilities that come with it and propose to follow them up in their training. If I do this today in my ministry, it's because someone – like the author of this book! – did the same for me one day.

CHAPTER 5

STOP! WEVE GOT SOMETHING TO TELL YOU!

The evangelist's message

The evangelist's job is to share the Good News: Jesus Christ died for our sins. He rose from the dead according to the Scriptures. He reigns as Lord, and to all those who repent and believe, he offers the forgiveness of sins and the gift of the Holy Spirit. That is good news!

How many of our peers have heard this good news? When we look at different surveys that have been taken, we quickly observe that people, and this is definitely the case in France, often have a rather exotic view of Christianity. It's not any different in Quebec. I remember once when we were doing a kind of 'sidewalk talk show' with people during the celebration of the 400th anniversary of the founding of the city of Quebec.

"When I say 'Saint-Laurent', you say... ?"

"Quebec!"

"When I say 'Eiffel Tower', you say... ?"

"Paris."

"God?"

"Clouds."

"Bible?"

"Myths"

"Jesus?"

"Doesn't exist."

That really happened. Stop! We've got something to tell you! And it's not at all what you think it is.

OUR MESSAGE IS POWERFUL!

The apostle Paul said: "For I am not ashamed of the gospel, for it is the power [*dunamis*] of God for salvation to everyone who believes" (Romans 1:16).

> The Gospel (Gr. *euaggelion* or *kerygma*) is centered on the person and work of Jesus Christ (Acts 5:42; 8:35; 28:31). For the Jews, the Gospel is the good news of the accomplishment of God's promises in the Old Testament (Acts 2:22-36; 3:13-25). For those outside of Judaism, it is the good news of the inauguration of a new kingdom, a kingdom of peace which was purchased through Christ's victory over Satan at the cross (Col 2:15). This proclamation of the *euaggelion* does more than simply announce the coming kingdom, it actually brings it about as a result of its intrinsic power. The Gospel is not a human invention: it is the Word of God (1 Pet 1:12) which brings about new birth (1 Pet 1:23-25). "The Gospel is not just a testimony to the salvation story; it is

> the salvation story." Therefore, the power of the Gospel is not to be found in the messenger, but in the message, which is the power [*dunamis*] of God for the salvation of anyone who believes.[1]

The evangelist must comprehend this doctrinal reality. The Gospel is not only powerful, it is also sufficient, in and of itself, to generate life in the heart of its hearer by the Holy Spirit.

THE DIFFERENT PERSPECTIVES OF THE EVANGELIST'S MESSAGE

Knowing this, the evangelist must be sure to work out his message from four different perspectives: Theology (content), confrontation (decision), apologetics (reasoning), and communication (adaptability).[2]

1. The message from the theological perspective

To understand the core of the theological perspective, one must grasp the very essence of the message we preach. My friend Michael Ramsden has spent much time developing what he calls the "ontological root of the Gospel."[3] With his authorization, I am using here his material.

The Gospel is powerful because it finds its anchor in the

[1]Raphaël Anzenberger, "Evangélisation (historique et pratique)," in *Dictionnaire de théologie pratique,* 325.

[2]Here I am indebted to the work of Alain Stamp on the development of the evangelist.

[3]Michael Ramsden, "Understanding The Root Of The Gospel And Finality," in *Vital Connections* (Oxford: RZIM, 2007)

person of Jesus Christ – "in Him." That is why Paul wrote to Timothy: "But I am not ashamed, for I know *whom* I have believed" (1 Timothy 1:12, *italics added*). The Gospel that we proclaim finds its source in the very person of God.[4] Ramsden reminds us that this is played out in the way that Jesus reveals himself, saves and transforms us.

The revelation of God in Christ

Jesus didn't come to tell us things about God. He is God in person. He who has seen the Christ has seen the Father (John 14:7). And because he is God he was able to accomplish the ministry that his Father had entrusted to him (Hebrews 10:5-7). His words and his actions flowed out from his divine nature. What Jesus came to do could not have been done by an angel, or even an archangel.

But that's not all: By his incarnation, he became one of us, a son of Adam, descendant of the line of David "according to the flesh," (Romans 1:3; 8:3; 2 Timothy 2:8) having taken on himself our humanity, the very essence of our existence.

God's salvation through Christ

It is through Jesus' physical death and resurrection that we are saved. These events are the essence of the *kerygma* that we proclaim.

It is because Jesus Christ became "sin for us," because he took our transgressions upon himself, that we are justified (2 Corinthians 5:21). He became what he wasn't, so

[4]Ramsden explains that the Gospel starts at an ontological root, unlike other religions that start from knowledge (orthodoxy) or practicing (orthopraxy). Christianity starts from ontology and results in orthodoxy and orthopraxy.

that we could become what we weren't. As Irenaeus of Lyon reminds us:

> For it behooved Him who was to destroy sin, and redeem man under the power of death, that He should Himself be made that very same thing which he was, that is, man; who had been drawn by sin into bondage, but was held by death, so that sin should be destroyed by man, and man should go forth from death.
>
> *Adversus Hoereses, III, 18, 7*

Jesus, the infinite God-man, bore an infinite number of sins on the cross. As he hung there, suspended between the earth and the heavens, he was cursed by God for our sins. Jesus was our substitute.[5] He who had never known what it was to sin became sin, so that we could become righteousness in him.

Christ's work of sanctification on our behalf

Jesus reminded Nicodemus that "... unless one is born again he cannot see the kingdom of God" (John 3:3). The fundamental problem facing a fallen humanity is not a lack of theological knowledge, as Muslims believe. Neither is it a faulty life ethic, as Buddhists believe. Mankind's main problem is that it is spiritually dead, eternally separated from God. If a man is to be truly alive, he must be born again by the Spirit of God. Ravi Zacharias, who is passionate about the theology of the Gospel message, loves to remind his hearers: "Morality is not the starting point or the finality of salvation. The Son of

[5]The doctrine of penal substitution is at the core of the Christianity contrary to ethical compensation where salvation is earned.

Man did not die on the cross so that bad people could become good, but that dead people could become alive. It's not the same thing!" (taken from one of his sermons)

When someone responds to the Gospel, he is born from on high (1 John 3:9), the seed of corruption loses its power and the renewed man brings forth the fruit of a new life. The Gospel we proclaim is therefore more than just an escape from the punishment of sin. As David Shutes reminds us:

> [...] many Christians reduce the entire gospel message to this: "Believe in Jesus, so that you can be forgiven and have eternal life." Pursuing holiness is usually regarded as an option for the super spiritual, rather than the very nature of the gospel. It is relatively easy to convince people to accept Jesus in order to escape the punishment for their sins. It is much harder to convince them of their need to be delivered from sin itself.[6]

The sinner who has passed from spiritual death to life discovers a new reality, the eschatological tension between "saved" and "glorified." It's only in the midst of this tension that this earthly life can be fully lived out.

In a nutshell

The Gospel we proclaim is therefore centered on the person of Jesus Christ and his works. Jesus Christ is both the Son of God and the Son of Man. One hundred percent divine so that he is without sin; one hundred percent human so that he could become our sin. Jesus saved us from the *condemnation*

[6]David Shutes, "Two Gospels: The gospel of man or the gospel of Jesus Christ?," June 2013, http://www.davidshutes.fr/?post_type=document&p=212 (Accessed 20 Feb 2014)

of sin through his death on the Cross (past), he saves us from the *power* of sin by the work of the Holy Spirit (present) and one day he will save from the *presence* of sin when we will be with him (future).

Every time I hear the Gospel message anew, I am amazed…

Stop! We have something to tell you! And it's not at all what you think!

The evangelist must be clear as to the theology of the message he is sharing. It is vital that he remain faithful to the *kerygma*. Otherwise, no seed of incorruptibility will be sown in the hearts of his hearers.

2. The message from the confrontational perspective

Article 4 of the Lausanne Covenant tells us that the evangelist is to share the Gospel "with a view to persuading people to come to him personally and so be reconciled to God." He must remain faithful to the theological content of his message, but he must also take pains to persuade his hearers to respond to his message.

When the Gospel is proclaimed, it is received either as a fragrance of life or a fragrance of death. A fragrance of life for some, as they go from death to life through the miracle of the new birth; a fragrance of death for others:

> For we are the aroma of Christ to God among those who are being saved and among those who are perishing, to one a fragrance from death to death, to the other a fragrance from life to life. Who is sufficient for these things? For we are not, like so many, peddlers of God's word, but

as men of sincerity, as commissioned by God, in the sight of God we speak in Christ. (2 Corinthians 2:15-17)

Evangelists may be tempted to "corrupt the Word of God" (KJV) by failing to share the eternal consequences which are a result of rejecting Christ. The reality is that the Scriptures give us an ultimatum. There is no other choice so we might as well be honest with people right away.

In his evangelism, Jesus confronted people. "No, I tell you; but unless you repent, you will all likewise perish" (Luke 13:3). "He said to them, 'You are from below; I am from above. You are of this world; I am not of this world. I told you that you would die in your sins, for unless you believe that I am he you will die in your sins'" (John 8:23, 24).

Peter also confronted his hearers: "Repent therefore, and turn back, that your sins may be blotted out" (Acts 3:19).

And of course, Paul never hesitated to use persuasion in his message. When he appeared before King Agrippa, he shared how he had "declared first to those in Damascus, then in Jerusalem and throughout all the region of Judea, and also to the Gentiles, that they should repent and turn to God, performing deeds in keeping with their repentance" (Acts 26:20).

What about me? Do I persuade my hearers to be reconciled with God? Do I bring them to the point where they can make a decision?

My friend and colleague Florent Varak is a real example to me in this area. When he preaches the Gospel, he doesn't hold anything back. Of course he includes the message of the *kerygma*, but he doesn't stop there. He always reminds his audience of the choice they have to make: Life... or death.

It's clear because the Gospel is clear, and it's powerful because the Gospel is powerful. Some people hear it as a fragrance of death which leads them to death, others, as a fragrance of life which leads them to life. Our responsibility is to bring the person to the place where he or she can actually make the choice; the rest is up to God.

The evangelist must be sure that his message is theologically sound, but he must never hesitate to make it confrontational. The two go hand in hand. If I proclaim the Gospel without confronting my hearers to make a decision, then I haven't fully "evangelized."

3. The message from the communication perspective

When we communicate the Gospel, we need to look at two aspects: The style of our message and the medium by which we choose to communicate it.

Adapt the style of your message

British evangelist J. John is extremely gifted at adapting his message to fit his audience, without ever compromising the *kerygma*. For example, when he preaches at large youth gatherings before thousands of young people seated on the ground in their sleeping bags, he shares the Gospel using this simple method:

"The Gospel message is a full forgiveness for your past, a new life for today and a hope for tomorrow."

I love it! It's theologically sound and confrontational in nature.

Another example: When he preaches to "Christmas and Easter Christians," he uses the Ten Commandments as a basis for his message, since traditional Christians are sensitive to the importance of obedience. He calls his message Just 10.

1st commandment:	Find contentment
2nd commandment:	Hold to the truth
3rd commandment:	Prosper with a clear conscience
4th commandment:	Affair-proof your relationship
5th commandment:	Manage your anger
6th commandment:	Keep the peace with your parents
7th commandment:	Catch your breath
8th commandment:	Take God seriously
9th commandment:	Know God
10th commandment:	Live by priorities

Everywhere he goes, J. John attracts hundreds of people to his message. Many joyfully turn to Christ each evening. He knows how to adapt his message to his hearers.

Vary the medium you use for the message

In our organization, we explore different mediums to see which ones are most effective as we share the Good News. Historically, we have been drawn to preaching the message in front of an audience. We are familiar with this medium and we have worked to perfect it.

When Alain Stamp became the president of our organization, he encouraged each of us to write a book on evangelism. Writing a book is nothing like preaching the Gospel. It's a new medium for us. Writing and preaching are two different things, which call for two different techniques.

Emmanuel Maennlein loves videos. He has already produced several evangelistic videos (7 Keys to Discovering Jesus, etc.) Every time I see him, he's working on a new one!

I started a format called Veritas Dialogues in a college ministry in 2006. Since then, we have organized over 100 Veritas evenings where we strive to answer college students' most pressing questions about God.

Saotra Rajaobelina likes to use blogs and videos to do mass distribution of the Gospel message using social networks.

One message, many mediums. Every evangelist must carefully consider the format he will use. But remember, the medium is not the only thing to consider, it is also important to be sure that the message is communicated in a way that will catch the listener's attention.

4. The message from an apologetic perspective

My homiletics professor Roy King was constantly encouraging us to read books dealing with subjects other than theology. That would be surprising coming from a seminary professor, but not from a homiletics professor.

An evangelist must know his audience. The best way to get to know your public is to read what they are reading. Since I graduated, I've made it a practice to stop in the bookstore every time I take a train. I read bestselling novels, books on spirituality, philosophy magazines, etc. It's expensive but it really helps me relate to the people I'm talking to.

The evangelist must constantly ask himself, "What is the point of contact between me and my listener?" Personally,

I like to use current events as a springboard: When do you think the financial crisis will end? Do you think the end of the world is near? Why are some religions so violent? When I bring these subjects up, I'm almost sure to connect with the person in some way. I consider this a crucial step in identifying with the person.

Once this connection is made, I try to start up a discussion with the person. I identify the point of tension, present the biblical perspective on the matter and attempt to overturn any false reasoning on the person's part.

After this, it's only natural to invite the person to respond to the message and make a decision for Christ. The person is confronted with the message, now it's up to him to make a decision.

Identification, argumentation, invitation.[7]

Ravi Zacharias often reminds us that "apologetics is trimming the bushes of doubt so that the skeptic can have a good look at the cross." It is essential that the evangelist look at the apologetic perspective of his message in order to connect with the public.

Theology, confrontation, communication and apologetics. Four different perspectives on the evangelist's message.

[7]Thanks to Richard Cunningham for sharing this useful apologetic technic!

IN CONCLUSION

The evangelist may feel intimidated when faced with all of these different angles. The apostle Paul asked himself, "Who is sufficient for these things?" (2 Corinthians 2:16). He gives us the answer a few verses later: "Not that we are sufficient in ourselves to claim anything as coming from us, but our sufficiency is from God" (2 Corinthians 3:5). It is God who qualifies the evangelist for proclaiming his message.

I am currently mentoring several young evangelists in their preaching ministry. After each message that they preach, we sit down to go over what happened. Oftentimes, we don't see any visible fruit from what has been shared, at least not on the surface. But our conversations may go something like this:

"I messed up this morning, I just wasn't feeling it."

"Hey, where does the power come from, my friend?"

"I know, but I just wasn't up to it this morning."

"Where does the power come from, my friend?"

"I should have worked on it more."

"Where does the power come from, my friend?"

"I don't even know anymore…"

"It comes from God… get that through your head!"

DIGGING DEEPER

Interview with **Marc Van de Wouwer**, *evangelist, preacher, author and conference speaker*

How can we adapt our evangelism to today's audience without compromising the content of the Gospel message?

Communicating an unchanging Gospel in an ever-changing world is definitely one of our greatest challenges! I like how John Stott talks about "double listening," which basically comes down to listening to the Word of God while remaining sensitive to the culture around us. We need to listen to God's Word in order to be filled with his thoughts, his teachings and his life. We need to listen to our society to know what people believe, what they think, what they are interested in, their needs, their suffering in order to identify biblical answers to their questions. Our goal is to find contact points to build aqueducts through which the living waters of Jesus Christ can flow directly to thirsty hearts.

Practically speaking, we follow Jesus' example. We need to take people's needs into consideration, and build from their side of the river. Listen before speaking. Since we live in a visual age, we shouldn't hesitate to use imagery in our explanations or to invent our own parables. We must communicate simply (people are no longer familiar with the Gospel as they once were), and deeply (with the whole Gospel), using the

Gospel as a mirror for what people are really living. We speak to their spirit but also to their heart.

To summarize, it's not the Gospel but we who need to adapt. We don't need to modernize Jesus' message, we need to come back to it!

Make no mistake about it, even when our technique is perfect, communicating the Gospel is hard work, and more and more so as time goes on. Even though it is the most beautiful message known to man, it calls forth a tsunami in people's consciousness. What we really need is courage!

What advice would you give to a young evangelist on how to deal with a world which is increasingly hostile to the Gospel message?

First of all, I would tell him he is one of the privileged few!

The communication of the Gospel has the power to change lives for eternity and is therefore the noblest of calls. No other message contains such power. But it's also an extremely demanding call. The Gospel has always met with opposition. Jesus and his disciples were constantly confronted with it and ultimately gave their lives for it. Still today, in many places, Christians risk their lives every day to share their faith. It is only in the Western world that social hostility toward the Gospel is something of a novelty. We just need to get used to it and remember that Jesus' love is the answer to this opposition.

Don't place your focus on the hostile masses, but concentrate your attention on the person in front of you and his spiritual needs. Find your satisfaction in the wonder of each new life touched and transformed by Jesus Christ. Don't seek the adulation of the crowds, but rather the deep and abiding change in each individual person's life.

When faced with criticism (and let's admit it, some of it is justified!), your message must be genuine and your personal integrity intact. Sometimes we hear a message which is straight out of the textbook, but the person is living a hypocritical life. Yes, the content of message is important, but so is the messenger!

Endurance and patience are necessary if you want to see fruit in your ministry. These character traits will be cultivated in your personal relationship with Jesus. Don't deprive Jesus of your daily presence, or you might be deprived of His!

It is essential to maintain and develop a healthy marital and family life if you want to persevere in the ministry. Also, don't forget the importance of sports and times of relaxation to help you deal with stress.

Above all else, Hebrews 12:1-3 reminds us to keep our eyes on Jesus! He has been through it all, without becoming discouraged or giving up. Don't forget that he's the one who called you, and he will be with you until the end.

CHAPTER 6

WHERE IS THE EVANGELIST'S PLACE IN THE LOCAL CHURCH'S STAFF?

Including the ministry of evangelist in the organizational flow chart

You may not believe it, but this question has been haunting me for over ten years.

We know where the pastor fits into the church flow chart (at the top), as well as the elders (at the top, next to or under the pastor, depending on your denomination). We know where to put the deacons, the Sunday school teachers and the youth workers. But what do we do with the evangelist?

Every time I meet with an experienced evangelist, I ask him:

"Where does the evangelist fit into the local church, and what is his role?"

And every time, he looks at me, perplexed, and says:

"That's an excellent question. You should do some research on the subject!"

But it's even worse when I visit a local church and I ask the pastor:

"Where are your evangelists?"

And he answers:

"Oh, didn't you know? We don't have any evangelists on staff in our church."

I hope this chapter will help us answer these questions. It might get a little bit technical, but I think it will be useful in giving us a more biblical, theological and missiological answer to the overwhelming deficit in the areas of recognition and positioning of evangelists in our local churches.

A BIT OF HISTORY

As we look back on the historical evolution of the ministry of the evangelist, we can see why it suffers from a lack of recognition in the local church today.

Let's start at the beginning. Kevin Giles observes that in the New Testament, charismatic-type ministries (such as evangelists) and institutional-type ministries (such as the role of elders or deacons) were often juxtaposed. Giles reminds us that the two structural styles (charismatic and institutional) are not opposed. Rather, they emphasize different areas of ministry.

> The earliest letters of Paul and the Johannine writings bear witness to an entirely Spirit-initiated ministry given by prophets, tongues speakers and others as the Spirit empowers; Luke, James, 1 Peter and the Pastoral Epistles, in contrast, bear witness to an institutional

order in which office bearers, notably elders, rule the church.[1]

Missiologist David Bosch has come up with the same conclusion:

> At an early stage there were indications of two separate types of ministry developing: the settled ministry of bishops (or elders) and deacons, and the mobile ministry of the apostles, prophets, and evangelists. The first tended to push early Christianity toward becoming an institution; the second retained the dynamic of a movement. In the early years in Antioch there was still a creative tension between these two types of ministry. Paul and Barnabas were at the same time leaders in the local church and itinerant missionaries, and apparently they resumed their congregational duties as a matter of course whenever they returned to Antioch.[2]

During the second century, Eusebius testified that "There were still many evangelists of the Word eager to use their inspired zeal after the example of the apostles for the increase and building up of the divine Word.[3]" The *Didache* also mentions the juxtaposition of sedentary and itinerant ministries, which seems to point to a certain continuity of the model given in the book of Acts.

However, when faced with heresies which threatened the understanding of sound doctrine, the Church began to

[1]Kevin Giles, "Church Order, Government," in Dictionary of the later New Testament and its developments.

[2]Bosch, 51.

[3]Michael Green, *Evangelism in the early Church*, 238.

develop its institutional facet on a deeper level. Giles points us to the writings of Ignatius:

> We read of a clearly defined threefold church order in which monarchical episcopacy is the most important element. Center stage stands the bishop, the unquestioned leader of the Christian community in a given city, who presides over a council of elders and is assisted by a group of deacons.[4]

J. A. Robinson observes that during this transitional period:

> the Christian Ministry was gradually evolved, in response to fresh needs which came with new conditions, as the Church grew in numbers and enlarged its geographical boundaries. We find that a Threefold Ministry emerges, which has proved itself capable of satisfying the wants of the Christian Church from the second century forward to the present day... It is for the unity of the whole that the Historic Threefold Ministry stands. It grew out of the need for preservation of unity when the Apostles themselves were withdrawn.[5]

This sort of "monarchical institutionalization" of the church (bishops, elders, deacons) continued well into the third century. The Franks were the first to organize their church life around priests, who were named over different

[4]Kevin Giles, "Church Order, Government," in Dictionary of the later New Testament and its developments.

[5]Joseph Robinson, "The Christian ministry in the apostolic and sub-apostolic periods". In Essays on the early history of the Church and the ministry, H. B. Swete (ed.), p. 57-92. London: Macmillan & Co., 1918, p. 92.

communities, under the supervision of a bishop for each diocese. It was at this time that the evangelist seemed to disappear from the pages of our history books...

We come upon him once again during the Reformation period. The Anabaptists began to question the idea of a geographically structured Christianity, with its parishes and dioceses. They saw the whole world as a mission field. They sent missionaries out onto the European continent, which did not meet with the approval of the Protestant reformers. Luther, especially, refused to recognize the legitimacy of any ministry which did not have strong local church ties. Evangelists in those days needed to be made of solid stuff![6]

John Calvin pushed the argument one step further as he questioned whether the evangelist's ministry had any regular place in the church. He wrote:

> Those who preside over the government of the Church, according to the institution of Christ, are named by Paul: first, apostles; second, prophets; third, evangelists; fourth, pastors; and fifth, Teachers (Eph. 4:11). Of these, only the two last have an ordinary office in the Church. The Lord raised up the other three at the beginning of his kingdom, and still occasionally raises them up when the necessity of the times requires. [...] According to this interpretation, which appears to me consonant both to the words and the meaning of Paul, those three functions were not instituted in the Church to be perpetual, but only to endure so long as churches were to be formed where none previously existed, or at least where

[6]David Bosch, *Transforming mission* (Maryknoll: Orbis Books, 2008), 246

> churches were to be transferred from Moses to Christ; although I deny not, that afterward God occasionally raised up apostles, or at least evangelists, in their stead, as has been done in our time. […] The office I nevertheless call extraordinary, because it has no place in churches duly constituted. Next come pastors and teachers, with whom the Church never can dispense… [7]

In a duly constituted church therefore, pastors and teachers took the forefront. The evangelist assumed a discreet role, seeking to exist in an ordinary, as opposed to extraordinary, fashion. He no longer operated under the authority of the local church, but rather under the direction of different mission societies, which, in the 19th century, opened the way for modern missions. This movement reached its peak in the 20th century, where more evangelistic organizations (like Campus Crusade for Christ, the Billy Graham Association, Operation Mobilization, etc.) were created in the last 50 years than in all of history since the beginning of Christianity.

In order to survive, the evangelist was forced to "take refuge" in various parachurch organizations which filled the role of the itinerant charismatic ministries of the 1st century. But the creative synergy is lost. The juxtaposition of local churches and Christian organizations today resembles a fractured structure more than an actual symbiosis of ministries. Patrick Johnstone, founder of Operation World, deplores this fact:

> I am here telling exactly what I think is one of the main reasons why the Church has failed to put into

---

[7]Jean Calvin, Institute of the Christian Religion, IV.3.4

> practice the last command of our Lord Jesus Christ. It is a structural issue. Throughout Church History, the lack of structural harmony or the distortion of existing structures has paralyzed our obedience to that fundamental command.[8]

So, what's the answer? Should we abandon any efforts to reconstruct a viable cooperation between ministries? I don't think so; I think there is a solution to the problem.

LET'S GET OUR DUCKS IN A ROW, PLEASE!

Now that we've looked at the historical reasons which led the evangelist away from the local church, all we need to do is reinvent a local church model where he can be welcomed back into the fold in an official manner, and exercise his ministry in a legitimate fashion. But, if you can just be patient a little bit longer, we need to clear up one more detail regarding the role of ministries in the church, and answer the question that you're all asking yourselves: "Where does the evangelist fit in the organization of the local church staff?"

Towards a better understanding of ministry in the local church

In order to extricate ourselves from this historical dead end, it is essential to rethink the relationship between the offices and the functions (or gifts) that Christ gave to the universal Church.

---

[8]Patrick Johnstone, *The church is bigger than you think: Structures and strategies for the church in the 21st century* (Fearn: Christian Focus Publications, 1998), 149

Harold Hoehner sheds some light on the subject:

> [...] it should be noted that those who hold offices are either appointed (Acts 14:23; Titus 1:5) or elected based on qualifications (Acts 1:26; 6:3; 1 Tim 3:1-13), whereas gifts are sovereignly bestowed directly by God (Eph 4:7; Rom 12:6; 1 Cor 12:11, 18, 28). Hence, there are no qualifications listed in any of the gifts passages. People are not given gifts based on observable qualifications but because of God's sovereign gracious act.[9]

We can infer several things from Hoehner's words:

First, while anyone can aspire to the office of an elder or a deacon (according to the democratic process of the local church), only certain individuals have been given to the church as evangelists, apostles, prophets or pastor-teachers (according to God's election in the universal Church).

Second, although the office of elder seems to be reserved for men, we do not find any such restrictions when it comes to spiritual gifts (cf. Ephesians 4:11; Romans 12:6; 1 Corinthians 12:11, 18, 28). As Hoehner says, "People are not given gifts based on observable qualifications but because of God's sovereign gracious act."

Can women be evangelists or Bible teachers? I believe they can. The question of female pastors is a bit more complicated. First of all, because separating the pastoral function from the teacher function in Ephesians 4:11 is an exegetical choice. If there is indeed a separation between the two, it is clear that in some church traditions the office of elder and the

[9]Harold Hoehner, "Can a woman be a pastor-teacher?" *Journal of the evangelical theological society*, December 2007, 50/4, p. 761-71, p. 764.

pastoral function are one and the same. In addition to the biblical qualifications for an elder, the church will therefore seeks individuals who possess a spiritual gift mix allowing them to assume the function of a pastor. Consequently, we can understand the restrictions placed on women which would keep them from the pastorate. But do we need to impose the same restrictions on women concerning the role of evangelist? To say that an evangelist must have all of the qualifications of an elder, thus excluding women from the ministry of the evangelist seems to me misplaced and even dangerous. Furthermore, different cultures have different ways of recognizing women in the ministry. For example, in Burkina Faso, the Assemblies of God recognize female evangelists, whereas in France, the same denomination denies that there is such a thing as an evangelist.

Third, the evangelist does not appear on the church's organizational flow chart in the same way that the elders or the deacons do. Missiologist Ronald Fung explains that the "'Office' is here thought of as a formally recognized position with appropriate duties, and 'function' as the discharge of a ministry without a formal position being involved."[10] Indeed, the evangelist is recognized for his ministry (cf. Chapter 2 for the ministerial qualifications of the evangelist) whereas elders and deacons are elected on the basis of character traits and qualities according to certain specifications which are given them by the local church. It is right therefore, that the local church differentiate between these two types of ministries.[11]

---

[10]Ronald Flung, "Function or office? A survey of the New Testament evidence," *Evangelical review of theology*, April 1984, Issue 8, p. 16-39, p. 16.

[11]A word of caution: differentiating does not necessarily imply strict segregation. One must keep a certain level of fluidity between the two spheres.

Finally, while it is true that the office of elder has existed since the Jewish tradition in Old Testament times, the different functions in the local church only appeared in the New Testament, after Pentecost.

Here's a table that might make things a little clearer:

<table>
<tr><th colspan="2"></th><th>OFFICE</th><th>FUNCTION</th></tr>
<tr><td colspan="2">Period</td><td>Old Testament
(Institutional
– Cultural)</td><td>New Testament
(Holy Spirit
– Pentecost)</td></tr>
<tr><td rowspan="4">MODE OF GOVERNMENT</td><td>Title</td><td>Elders
Deacons</td><td>Apostle
Prophet
Evangelist
Pastor-teacher</td></tr>
<tr><td>Who can aspire to this?</td><td>Anyone (1 Timothy 3, Titus 1)</td><td>Given by Christ
(Ephesians 4)</td></tr>
<tr><td>Qualifications?</td><td>Character traits</td><td>Call, confirmation, competency</td></tr>
<tr><td>Role of the Holy Spirit</td><td colspan="2">Gives spiritual gifts so the individual can exercise his office or his function (i.e. gift of wisdom, leadership, knowledge, etc.)</td></tr>
<tr><td colspan="2">Sphere of influence</td><td>Local church pastorate</td><td>Church development (from the church plant stage through to the building up of the church)</td></tr>
</table>

HOW DO WE PUT THIS INTO PRACTICE?

For those of us who live in the 21st century, our main concern is to return the ministry of evangelist to the local church without compromising biblical truth, all the while being sensitive to the role that history has played in its development. Even if, in the past few years, the ministry has flourished mainly in the framework of parachurch organizations, there is no reason that the local church can't get in on the action too!

Alexandre Tirman proposes four types of "structural repositioning" for the evangelist in the local church:

The local evangelist

Definition: An evangelist who works out of his or her local church.

Specifications: The individual must be a member of the local church, recognized as having the gift of the evangelist and be capable of taking the responsibility of the evangelism ministry in his local church. He might organize his ministry around a "pool of evangelists" which gathers other evangelists from within the local church. (cf. Interview with Florent Varak at the end of this chapter for more details on this local strategy).

Financing: His expenses (travel, administrative, etc.) should be reimbursed by the church when he is involved in local evangelism.

STRENGTHS	WEAKNESSES
• Because this evangelist often works somewhere near the local church, his impact on the local community is somewhat guaranteed.	• He is less available than a full-time evangelist. It takes seven to ten "volunteer evangelists" to make up the work of one full-timer. The local evangelist can usually give between three and five hours per week to the ministry. • It is difficult for the local church to invite an evangelist from outside the church if nothing has been set aside in the budget for that ministry.

Every local church has at least one brother or sister who has the gift of the evangelist. We need to keep our eyes open for these people and recognize them as such! According to Wagner and Schwartz, 10% of all church members are evangelists.[12] Let's start by recognizing their gifts, getting them plugged into the church and refusing the idea that they might divide the local church or, even worse, start a new one!

The revivalist evangelist

Definition: Depending on the local church's ecclesiastic tradition, this can be a missionary, a church planter or an apostle.

Specifications: A church planter's goal will be to create a new church, usually in cooperation with a team.

Sometimes when a new church is planted, after several years it may experience a time of stagnation. At this point a new evangelist may be called in to renew the church's vision. We wouldn't call this person a church planter, but rather, a revivalist.

Financing: This person can be a full-time employee of the church, or have a part-time job on the side.

STRENGTHS	WEAKNESSES
• Since the person lives in the same community as the local church, he can take advantage of his local contacts. • He can train the local church members in evangelism. • He is present at key moments in the church's development. • He benefits from a specific budget set aside for his ministry, according to the church's needs at any given moment.	• The evangelist is not a replacement for the pastor! Some people who feel that the pastor is not giving them enough attention may seek it from the evangelist and end up leaving the church when they don't get what they are looking for. • If the ministry of the "revivalist evangelist" is not well received by the church and encouraged by the leadership, the situation can become very tense for all involved.

[12]Rice Broocks' research brings this statistic down to 1% (Broocks, William Rice, Jr. 2010. "The Gift of the Evangelist." Fuller Theological Seminary, School of Intercultural Studies. Doctor of Missiology. 180 pp.)

It takes great courage and a finely-honed analytical strategy for a local church to realize that they need to "hire" a revivalist instead of a full-time pastor for a season in the church's development. It is very rare that we see a church which possesses this combination of insight and boldness.

The regional evangelist

Definition: Regional evangelist.

Specifications: The regional evangelist's task consists of developing the evangelistic ministry in several churches in a given region. His goal is not to exercise his gift through a base of relational contacts, but rather to encourage and develop evangelism in the surrounding communities through activities and events.

Financing: Working in conjunction with other churches lightens the financial load for everyone and can be a real encouragement for small churches who want to benefit from the presence of an evangelist.

STRENGTHS	WEAKNESSES
• Permanent presence of a regional evangelist. • Lighter financial burden for each local church involved. • If the evangelist has a part-time job, he will tend to be accepted more easily in the region.	• The evangelist often finds himself torn between the local churches he is working in. • He should not take on more than three churches. Any more than that and things tend to get complicated! • Juggling the different churches schedules can be a challenge!

It is essential that the churches who are 'sharing' the evangelist communicate so that they can prioritize his responsibilities and be very clear about each local church's expectations from the beginning. Otherwise, the evangelist may be tempted to cross the line and become some kind of part-time pastor, and this is not where his gifting lies.

The networking evangelist

Definition: An evangelistic consultant. The networking evangelist's ministry is similar to the work of a regional sales manager who travels from store to store analyzing, advising the on-site manager and acting as a link between employees. He is responsible for increasing the influence of evangelism within his network of churches.

Specifications: He is an expert in evangelism and development and is capable of conducting ministry "audits" on a regular basis. He counsels the church in the area of evangelism and accompanies the church leadership in developing the organization of the church towards an evangelistic ministry which is increasing both in quantity and in quality.

Financing: This evangelist may be hired to take care of the needs of an entire church movement. His salary is then covered by the denomination which has taken him on.

STRENGTHS	WEAKNESSES
• He helps all of the local churches in his network to grow in their vision for evangelism. • As he visits different churches, his knowledge and expertise are deepened. He is able to observe what works in one church and to share that with other churches. • He can have an influence on several churches at a time. • His salary is covered by several churches or by an entire denomination.	• He cannot necessarily guarantee a long-term presence in any given church plant. • He may find it difficult to correctly evaluate local particularities. • He may struggle to influence local church leaders who are often convinced that "their way is the best way". In order to succeed, he must be careful to approach things in a gentle and understanding manner.

Local churches need to reflect on the endless possibilities in this type of ministry! Church leaders often lack the objectivity needed to analyze the evangelistic ministry in their region. The regional evangelist is a specialist who knows how to analyze the local context, the church's history and its strengths and weaknesses in order to propose a working plan which will revitalize the local church growth.

IN CONCLUSION

You made it to the end of this chapter... congratulations! Now you can take an aspirin, go to bed and dream of the all sorts of evangelist breeds. We've come full circle; there is a solution to the problem of structural divorce between the local church and the ministry of the evangelist. The evangelist can finally take his rightful place in the church's organizational flow chart. Do you still need a little convincing?

In 2010, I attempted the impossible. I decided to plant a denominational church (France Mission), using evangelists from several different parachurch organizations (France Evangelization, Youth for Christ, the Navigators). It was one of the first times that evangelistic organizations decided to work together to actually plant a church. And you know what? It worked! When churches and parachurch organizations cooperate with each other on the basis of a mutual statement of faith, using healthy accountability structures, the apostolic genius begins to work again and everyone comes out a winner. Evangelists lead people to Christ and baptize them, the church grows and the denomination rejoices. Alan Hirsch says that when the evangelistic function is in sync with other ministries, it results in the "expansion of the faith through a response to God's personal call and organic numerical growth of the people of God."[13]

Putting these ideas into practice remains a challenge for churches, but we must not give up the fight. All things are possible! And the salvation of those around us depends on our success!

[13]Alan Hirsch, *The forgotten ways* (Grand Rapids: Brazos Press, 2006), 170.

DIGGING DEEPER

Interview with **Florent Varak,**
pastor, author, professor

Are you a pastor or an evangelist? Can you explain?

Sometimes I wonder! I try to be intentional in my friendships in order to develop occasions to share my faith. Leading someone to Christ is by far the greatest joy of my ministry.

In one way or another, the evangelist teaches, proclaims or dialogues around the theme of the Gospel. Therefore, evangelism should be a natural extension of the ministry of any pastor-teacher. Not all pastors have the same burden for evangelism, but they should all be involved in one way or another.

What is the role of the evangelist in your local church?

Until recently, we've always had an attitude of allowing those who are gifted in evangelism to exercise their gifts, while trying to encourage them from within the church leadership. Our evangelists are encouraged to bring their projects to fruition as the church comes alongside them to help where we can.

When one of our young people, Melissa, was a teenager, she had a burden to start a monthly evangelistic project in the streets of Lyon. When she brought this up to the youth group, several of them joined her in starting a week-long evangelistic camp called Light on the Street. We, as a church, rallied around the youth, encouraging them any way we could (prayer, meals, lodging, etc.).

Others have begun an outreach called "Take a Shot at the Pastor." They invite their unsaved friends over for a fun evening of snacks and drinks, including a ten minute speech by the pastor, followed by a time of Q & A. Of course, no subject is taboo, and all questions are encouraged.

We also have a group of people who have joined an outreach to local prostitutes.

And lastly, we have developed a series of Discovery Bible studies which are very user-friendly. Every year, several Discovery Bible studies take place with non-Christians. We get together in bars, in people's homes – hardly ever at the church.

One crucial factor has been the fact that the elders in our church are willing to take risks. They have embraced the possibility that a ministry may fail, or that people who are not 100% prepared might take on one of these ministries.

For the past year, we have been trying something new. We have begun different 'hubs' within our local church in an attempt to gather people with similar spiritual gifts in order to encourage them in the development of their ministries. But I've noticed that we have a tendency to slip very quickly from actual evangelism into a sort of "evangelistic activity." While it's true that evangelistic events or activities have their place, we need to be careful not to simply become an evangelistic committee. We need to maintain the evangelist's vision for the unsaved world, and take advantage of any opportunity available to share Christ in a creative and Spirit-led way.

How do you train your evangelists?

We have used several different formats and tools (especially BILD courses[14]). But I've noticed that an evangelist's authority and impact are not always the fruit of his or her training. The evangelist's life, his authenticity and his faith are so important. I'm more and more convinced that the best training for an evangelist takes place in the simplicity of the local church. When we provide a worship service where the non-Christian feels comfortable, along with Bible teaching which includes all of the counsel of God with an emphasis on the Gospel, I believe this to be an excellent training ground for our evangelists.

We have also begun a local Bible institute which aims to give basic training to those who have the gift of the evangelist. We have found that once individuals have followed the classes on evangelism, apologetics and leading a Discovery Bible study, they are fairly confident and competent to go out on their own.

How does evangelism work in conjunction with other ministries in your local church (pastoral ministries, teaching, etc.)?

I admit there are tense moments sometimes! I believe the ministry of the evangelist to be of the utmost importance. In my mind, it comes before the ministry of pastor or teacher (at least that's what Ephesians 4 tells us). But I know that it is often seen in a negative light, and is not given its rightful place in the church. On the other hand, hardcore evangelists can be pretty cynical regarding other facets of local church life,

[14]See http://www.bild.org

finding them to be "cold" and accusing people of being in a rut if they are not involved in evangelism.

As I write these words, I realize that we as a Church at large have not done all that we should have to identify and publicly encourage evangelists. This might explain the tensions that we feel sometimes.

Does your church do much evangelistic networking?

Not really. I've noticed, whether it's a good thing or a bad one, that personal connections and trust play a huge part in our relationships with unbelievers. It's really hard to invite an evangelist to come for an event in the local church without him having built some kind of trust relationship with Christians first of all, and before they will even think about inviting their non-Christian friends.

We have participated in some evangelistic campaigns in cooperation with other churches in the greater Lyon area. This has allowed us to encourage a more dynamic evangelistic ministry in our own church, to publicly announce the Gospel and to put our resources to use with other like-minded churches in our city.

How do you integrate seekers into your church?

Every Sunday, we ask newcomers to stand and introduce themselves. We give them a welcome packet which explains who we are as a church, as well as a Gospel presentation. If they've come with friends, we encourage them to do a Discovery Bible study together, and I make sure their Christian friends are able to lead the study themselves. If not, I'm available to help them in that area. Once a person is saved, their friends prepare them for baptism. One of my greatest joys is to witness someone being baptized by the person who led him or her to Christ! And lastly, we encourage our new believers to become part of a house church and also to see where they can serve in the local church as a whole.

What advice would you give a pastor who wants to revitalize the evangelistic ministry in his local church?

He's got to start with himself. We can't pass the spark on to anyone else if we aren't on fire ourselves. I would advise him to spend time every week in local cafés, on the bus, at the mall – anywhere people are gathered – and pray for those people. Pray for courage, pray for ideas, pray for a renewed compassion.

Then, I would propose that he follow the same format that we propose in our church:

Who? Specific and regular intercession.

- weekly prayer times as a family
- set an alarm to go off at the same time every day and pray for those God has given you a burden for, etc.

How? Develop authentic relationships.

- acts of service
- hospitality
- activities
- cookouts, etc.

What? Embrace my Christian identity.

- talk about the Bible
- pray before meals in public
- invite someone to church, etc.

Which tools do I want to use? Explain the Gospel.

- John 3:16
- Romans 3:23-25
- Ephesians 2:1-10
- Luke 15
- Discovery Bible study, etc.

If a pastor begins to renew his own passion for witnessing, he'll talk about it with others, and they will be inspired by his passion, and will begin witnessing themselves. Isn't that what discipleship is all about?

CHAPTER 7

WHAT DO I DO WITH MY EVANGELIST?

Training the budding evangelist

Hello Raphael,

We've got someone in our church who seems to be gifted in evangelism. How should we go about training him? Do you have any advice?

Thanks for your help,
Pastor Adams

I often receive letters from local church leaders who don't know what to do with up-and-coming evangelists in their churches. How can they tell if someone really has the gift of the evangelist? What kind of training should these people receive? How should they go about developing their ministry? The questions are endless, but we'll try to answer some of them in this chapter.

FROM RECOGNITION TO TRAINING & THE WEAKEST LINK

An evangelist's gift must be recognized by the local church (cf. Chapter 6) before any kind of ministry training can begin. His ministry cannot be developed on a local level without this type of support. Once a local body recognizes the gift of evangelist in one of its members, it will be more likely to want to invest in his training and give him the room he needs to exercise his ministry.

Research on our R2E[1] program shows that most of the applicants who come to us without any kind of theological training hope to prove to their local church that they do indeed have the gift of the evangelist. Their thinking runs along these lines: "If I can successfully complete this program, maybe my church will finally realize that God is calling me to be an evangelist."

This is backwards thinking.

On the other hand, all those who have joined R2E while actively pursuing theological studies at the same time have expressed the fact that their local church had already recognized them as an evangelist. This begs the question: Why do we jump at the chance to validate the call of an evangelist who is getting ready to head off to a Bible institute, but hesitate to recognize the call of another? Is a degree in theology a

[1]Translated *Emerging Evangelists Network.* The vision is to build a developing network of cutting edge young leaders in kingdom evangelism who through the program have been affirmed in their call, advanced in their character and spiritual growth and associated with other leaders. This program was first implemented in the US under Leighton Ford's leadership (The Sandy Ford Fellowship).

necessary prerequisite to being recognized as an evangelist? If so, what about the call that God may have given the person?

Missiologist David Bosch is a staunch defender of the idea that theological training should go hand in hand with practical ministry:

> The universal claim of the hermeneutics of language has to be challenged by a hermeneutic of the deed, since doing is more important than knowing or speaking. [...] There is, in fact, "no knowledge except in action itself, in the process of transforming the world through participation in history. [...] The relationship between theory and praxis is not one of subject to object, but one of intersubjectivity.[2]

In other words, an evangelist doesn't necessarily need to have completed his or her theological studies before being recognized as such by the local church, or before putting his or her gift into practice. Training and application go hand in hand. If an evangelist's theological training is to have any sense, it must be clearly recognized and lived out in the local church, and validated by tangible results.

THE SIX ELEMENTS OF TRAINING

If you take a quick look at what's being said about the training of evangelists (cf. Bibliography), you'll find six different elements which need to be taken into consideration in any program:

[2]David Bosch, *Transforming Mission*, 425.

1. Teaching by example

We see this modeled in the life of Christ, the greatest evangelist who ever lived.

During his three-year ministry, Jesus showed us what it means to cultivate relationships with others, to sow the Word of God in peoples' hearts, and to pray for an abundant harvest of souls.[3]

The art of relationships

Jesus constantly sought to be in contact with unbelievers. He developed quality relationships with people. He didn't see them as "contacts" or evangelistic projects, but as lost sheep in search of a shepherd. He helped them to realize their worth in God's eyes. He accepted them for who they were, and not for what they could do for him.

Spending time with non-Christians can wreak havoc on one's reputation. Jesus knew this, and he was willing to be misunderstood by his close friends and family, as well as by the religious leaders of his day. Simon the Pharisee spoke regarding Jesus, "If this man were a prophet, he would have known who and what sort of woman this is who is touching him, for she is a sinner" (Luke 7:39). It is extremely unfortunate to observe that those who tend to put a damper on evangelism are often church leaders themselves. Are we willing to welcome sinners into our midst? It's easy to say that we are, but it's another thing altogether to actually do it.

---

[3] I am indebted here to the work of my mentor Bill Jones, President of Columbia International University.

The art of sowing

Jesus took advantage of every possible occasion He had to sow the Word of God. He shared as he walked on the road to Emmaus, as he taught in the temple in Jerusalem. Morning, noon and night he spoke God's Word to the crowds who pressed around him, and with a lonely woman at a well. Jesus knew how to ask questions, the right questions. He always had the appropriate word for the occasion: "And all spoke well of him and marveled at the gracious words that were coming from his mouth. And they said, 'Is not this Joseph's son?'" (Luke 4:22). He also knew how to listen and discern peoples' needs: "When Jesus saw him lying there and knew that he had already been there a long time, he said to him, 'Do you want to be healed?'" (John 5:6). He didn't shy away from spiritual subjects, even though his listeners didn't always understand what He was talking about. How long do we wait to bring conversations around to spiritual things? Unfortunately, by the time we decide to do so, the occasion may be long past!

The art of harvesting

Jesus' passion was to see people saved: "O Jerusalem, Jerusalem, the city that kills the prophets and stones those who are sent to it! How often would I have gathered your children together as a hen gathers her brood under her wings, and you were not willing!" (Matthew23:37). He took advantage of all of His natural spheres of influence, whether through friends and family (Martha, Mary and Lazarus in Bethany), or through professional and social circles (by virtue of His position as rabbi). Jesus saw beyond the simple aspect of friendship; He knew when someone was ready to make a decision. Where the disciples saw a jar left at the side of a well, Jesus saw fields which were white unto harvest. "Look, I tell you, lift up your eyes, and see that the fields are white for harvest" (John 4:35). What do I see when I lift up my eyes?

If we want to train evangelists like Jesus did, our own example is the most important element. Is it radical? Yes, but it's also effective!

2. Investing with authority

If we want our evangelists-in-training to go out and change the world, we need to share with them all of the resources that are available to us, but also to invest them with the authority that accompanies their ministry.

This book was originally written in French. As I wrote it I realized that the French language doesn't have an equivalent for the English word "empower." When we empower someone that we are training, we communicate our power to them. In other words, we don't just give them the necessary resources to fulfill their ministry, but also the authority and legitimacy. While investing someone with a responsibility communicates the idea of authority, it doesn't necessarily communicate the sharing of resources.

The French are not the only ones to struggle with this concept. Jesus' disciples found themselves in the same boat. The Hebrew society was familiar with the idea of apprenticeship. Oftentimes, the apprentice would leave his home in order to learn a trade with a relative. This was the case with Lot and Abraham. Apprenticeship is a training method which dates back to the beginning of time. However, it was usually understood that the master would retain his position as master, and the apprentice would continue on in the subordinate position of apprentice. In other words, there has always been a distance between the teacher and the learner, so that the apprentice would never assume the position of his master. The latter guarded the essence of his expertise like a precious treasure, which in turn gave him a certain prestige. He was careful not to transmit this expertise to his apprentice.

The disciples must have been shocked when Jesus, their rabbi, their Master, said to them, "Truly, truly, I say to you, whoever believes in me will also do the works that I do; and greater works than these will he do, because I am going to the Father" (John 14:12)! Greater works than these! When Jesus sent his disciples into the world, he clothed them with the power of the Holy Spirit and gave them authority in his name. The whole package! The disciples were empowered! This was absolutely necessary in order for them to transform the known world, to the extent that some jealous Jews said, "These men who have turned the world upside down have come here also [...] and they are all acting against the decrees of Caesar, saying that there is another king, Jesus" (Acts 17:6).[4]

If Jesus was eager for his disciples to do greater works than his, we shouldn't be afraid to put all of our resources at our disciples' fingertips so that they can do greater things than we do, once and for all.

---

[4]To further the discussion, I strongly encourage reading Martin Sanders, *The Power of Mentoring: Shaping People Who Will Shape the World* (Camp Hill: Christian Publications, 2004).

3. Teaching doctrine

An evangelist must be capable to communicate the message of the Gospel faithfully according to the Scriptures. Evangelists are often looked down on when they adventure into the field of theology. We wish they would have taken the time to get a degree from a Bible institute like everyone else, and observe that they are prone to handle biblical texts lightly, sometimes going so far as to deform the meaning.

We need to take this criticism seriously. Otherwise, we run the risk of completely discrediting the wonderful ministry of the evangelist.

An evangelist dare not fear biblical doctrine. On the contrary! Theology, or theo-logos, is the language of God. We need to be speaking his language, no less and no more. If the evangelist wants to communicate the Gospel from the Scriptures, he must learn to understand the meaning of the text. This is what we call hermeneutics (the science of interpretation). Nothing complicated, just a healthy dose of practice to help him acquire a correct methodology which will allow him to study a passage in its context. This way, the text will become the basis for the message that he is burning to share.

It is imperative that the evangelist be grounded in his biblical theology if he wants to effectively share the Gospel. In other words, he needs to know how to correctly place the passage in its book, the book in with the other writings of the author, the author's writing in the whole of Scripture. Isaiah developed his theology in a certain way, as did John and especially Paul. We need to beware of the temptation to jump around from verse to verse with a concordance and think that we have acquired a solid systematic theology! Evangelists the world over need to confess this sin!

Hermeneutics, biblical theology... and dogma. In other words, we need to grasp the great theological topics of the Scriptures like soteriology (the study of salvation) or Christology (the study of the person of Christ). These subjects must be a part of the evangelist's doctrinal toolbox. Once these subjects are mastered, the evangelist will be able to effectively communicate the Gospel... the whole Gospel.

4. Teaching ethics

The message proclaimed by an evangelist is revolutionary, prophetic, radical (Chapter 5). His message is deep and powerful. But how many times has an evangelist's message been reduced to ashes as he himself is disqualified because of an ethical problem! As Ulrich Parzany reminded us in Chapter 3, "An evangelist devoid of character is a criminal!"

There are two subjects that are particularly sensitive and must be approached during an evangelist's training period: financial integrity and sexual integrity.

Financial integrity

The evangelist is often called upon to organize evangelistic projects which must be financed somehow. Sooner or later, an evangelist will have to deal with money. This is not a problem in and of itself. Jesus' evangelistic ministry was financed by the generosity of others through a common fund which provided for his needs. But when the woman anointed Jesus with expensive oil, the disciples were angry (Matt 26:6-13). This shows how our enemy Satan can use finances to trip us up in our evangelism. Werner Burklin[5] insists on the fact that financial integrity in one's personal life precedes financial integrity in the ministry. It is of the utmost importance. In other words, if the evangelist does not practice integrity in the way he manages his own finances, how can we expect him to manage the finances of others in an honorable fashion? During my evangelistic studies, I had to take an accounting class. Two columns: Credit and debit… some simple math, and you have your result. The evangelist doesn't need to have a degree in accounting, but he does need to have an idea of how to manage finances. Otherwise, the ministry should be turned over to someone else who can take care of it. In our organization we have the privilege of having a full-time accountant who keeps us on our toes financially. Thank God for Nathalie! But in the end, each one is responsible for his or her finances.

When working on an evangelistic project where you'll be dealing with amounts that reach more than $10,000, it's a good idea to have an auditor look at the financial side of things. His services come at a price, but it is also a guarantee of the project leader's financial irreproachability. Including the auditor's fees in the final cost of the project will save you from headaches down the road.

Sexual integrity

This is a subject that we French don't like to talk about. "My private life is none of your business," we say. But the Bible

[5]Werner Burklin, "The training and development of evangelists," in *The Mission of an Evangelist: Amsterdam, 2000,* ed. Douglas, J., 337-338. (Minneapolis: World Wide Publications, 2001), 337.

teaches that a person's private life reveals more about his or her true nature than their public *façade,* for "... out of the heart come evil thoughts, murder, adultery [*moicheiai*], sexual immorality [*porneiai*], theft, false witness, slander. These are what defile a person. But to eat with unwashed hands does not defile anyone" (Matthew 15:19-20).

Anyone who partakes of sexual relations outside of his or her couple, or who seduces a married person is an adulterer (*moicheia*). In either case, the Bible is clear: STOP! Jesus takes it even further: "But I say to you that everyone who looks at a woman with lustful intent has already committed adultery with her in his heart" (Matthew 5:28). He sets the bar high! Adulterous thoughts precede adulterous acts. It is absolutely crucial that we know how to bring every adulterous thought "captive to obey Christ" (2 Corinthians 10:5). For married evangelists: The sexual health of your couple will be a determining factor in your ministry. If you refuse to carefully consider this aspect of your life, you are taking risks that the enemy of your soul will not hesitate to exploit.

Immorality (*porneia*) is mentioned twenty-four times in the New Testament. Needless to say, God considers it an important subject. The root word conveys the idea of prostitution, but was used in ancient times as well as in Scripture to encompass all sorts of wanton sexuality. Pornography, for example, would fall under this category, and we don't need to be reminded of how this societal phenomenon has exploded since the introduction of the Internet. We must keep in mind that pornography is a top risk for any evangelist, male or female. The careful evangelist will be sure to be in an accountability relationship with someone they trust. The prayer of the psalmist will ring true in his heart:

> I will ponder the way that is blameless. Oh when will you come to me? I will walk with integrity of heart within my house; I will not set before my eyes anything that is worthless. I hate the work of those who fall away; it shall not cling to me. A perverse heart shall be far from me; I will know nothing of evil. (Psalm 101:2-4)

5. Teaching Biblical leadership

Evangelists often find themselves pushed to the front of the stage, figuratively speaking or literally. They're the ones who carry the torch for evangelism, who mobilize the saints so that the witness of the church can continue to increase. The evangelist is a passionate person. As we listen to him tell stories about the different people he's led to the Lord, we think to ourselves, "It sounds so easy! Why doesn't that happen to me?"

This is why it's so important that the evangelist fulfill his ministry in all humility, making sure that all of the glory goes to Jesus Christ. In order to do that, the evangelist needs to have a clear vision of what biblical leadership looks like.

Leighton Ford consecrated the majority of his adult life to training young evangelists. In his book, *Transforming Leadership,* he particularly emphasizes the transformational aspect of leadership in the life of the evangelist. All biblical leadership, he says, must find its source in an intimate relationship with the Father. The evangelist remembers that his heavenly Father is holy and sovereign, that he provides for his needs, forgives him and delivers him from evil (Matthew 6:9-13). Biblical leadership flows from a relationship with the Father, is anchored in the identity of the Son and walks in the power of the Spirit. From there, the transformational process of leadership can occur naturally, "from the inside out" as our young leaders like to remind us. When defined in this way, the biblical leader is not confined to a static role which delimits his identity and his ministry. On the contrary, since his identity is based on the person of God himself, his leadership role becomes flexible. On certain occasions he will act as a leader, while on another he may act as a follower, and neither of these will have any effect on his identity. Take, for example, my working relationship with fellow evangelist Alain Stamp. Our leadership is functional.[6] Sometimes he takes the lead in a project and I follow him (as president of France Evangelization). At other times, I'm up front and he's in the background (in my role as president of the Evangelists' Forum). Our roles are interchangeable.

This freedom to exchange leadership roles is only possible when we are convinced that our identity as a leader does not depend on our position or our responsibilities at any given moment. When we are willing to pay this price, we are ready to invest in the lives of young evangelists who will pattern their style of leadership *after* Jesus, *for* Jesus, in order to bring people *to* Jesus!

---

[6]For more insights on leadership as function, refer to Malakyan, Petros Grigor. 1998. *Christ-Like Leadership: Theological and Missiological Foundations for Leadership and Development (An Armenian Case Study)*. Fuller Theological Seminary, School of World Mission, Ph.D. Intercultural Studies, pp. 406.

6. Urging toward multiplication

Multiplication is the last element of training for your evangelist. We already spoke briefly on the subject in Chapter 4. It is the unequivocal condition for a visible and victorious ministry in evangelism.

Christian Schwarz has done vast amounts of research on missiology and is the author of the well-known book entitled *Natural Church Development.* He insists on the fact that growth in any structure is the result of six factors which he deems as "organic," one of which is reproduction or multiplication:

> The principle of multiplication applies to all areas of church life: Just as the true fruit of an apple tree is not an apple, but another tree, the true fruit of a small group is not a new Christian, but another group; the true fruit of a church is not a new group, but a new church. The true fruit of a leader is not a follower, but a new leader; the true fruit of an evangelist is not a convert but new evangelists.[7]

[7]Christian A. Schwarz, Natural Church Development (St. Charles: ChurchSmart Resources, 2000), 68.

Leighton Ford describes two types of leaders, comparing them to a banyan tree and an aspen.

- The banyan tree is majestic. So majestic that its leaves do not permit the slightest ray of sun to reach the earth below it. Nothing grows under a banyan tree. The banyan leader takes up all of the space around him; no one exists but him.
- The aspen's roots reach deep into the earth below him, where no one sees them. The largest aspen tree is in Colorado and has over forty-four thousand offshoots. Aspens are nowhere near as majestic as banyans, but what an amazing root system! The aspen leader is the one who works discreetly to multiply himself.

Whenever a local church asks me how they can revive the ministry of the evangelist in their midst, I always tell them, "Be aspen leaders! Figure out who the evangelists are in your church, recognize them as such and pour your life into them so that they, in turn, can reproduce their ministry in others. With an abundance of evangelists comes an abundance of evangelistic programs!" Be careful, it works every time!

IN CONCLUSION

The six elements of training (teaching by example, investing with authority, teaching doctrine, ethics and biblical leadership, and urging toward multiplication) have proven their worth over the years. These elements were the basis of Jesus' curriculum, so why would we want to do anything differently? No one is greater than his Master!

DIGGING DEEPER

Interview with **Raphael Anzenberger,**
evangelist and director of R2E,
an evangelistic training program in France.

What training strategy have you decided to follow at France Evangelization?

Historically speaking, France Evangelization (FE) has always required that any candidate for an evangelistic ministry complete three years of Bible institute. We have recently changed our recruitment strategy. Now we would consider God's call on an individual's life, his or her recognition by the local church, and the emergence of specific skills which are conducive to the proclamation of the Gospel as being more important. For example, our last two recruits joined FE without any prior theological training. They will be trained through an academic tutoring program for the first five years of their ministry. Keep in mind that the first two years of any candidate's ministry are "probationary." This allows us to observe and evaluate them in the areas we deem important (academics, character and competency). Although we don't require prior theological training, we certainly don't underestimate the importance of an excellent education. Our goal is that all of our evangelists earn at least a bachelor's degree in theology.

This program is innovative in that it associates mentoring

with academic tutoring in order to cover all the bases of the training process. In the mentoring relationship, the emphasis is placed on the candidate's character (teaching by example, investing with authority) and the transmission of different competencies (teaching biblical leadership, urging toward multiplication). The academic tutoring side of the program focuses on helping the young evangelist to obtain a solid theological foundation so that the message of the Gospel can be clearly communicated (teaching doctrine, teaching ethics). In this way the triad of "character, competency and knowledge" is developed at the same time through the mentoring relationship and the tutoring program.

In order to improve the quality of recruitment at FE, we have developed a "network of associates." We encourage anyone who wants to work with FE to join up with this group of budding evangelists for at least two years before coming to us. This way, they can become more familiar with the culture of our organization, and we can start getting to know them a little bit. Some of these associates have come out of our R2E program, which is the starting block for emerging evangelists. From R2E to the network of associates, then on to a full-time evangelist ministry with FE… that's our winning formula!

Is support-raising included in your training program?

When I decided to quit my job at Michelin to become a full-time evangelist, I was having a hard time finding financial support for my ministry. Alain Stamp told me, "Don't try to avoid the support-raising side of things. This is part of the evangelist's ministry too." We need to be sure that our candidates understand this aspect of ministry as well.

We encourage them right off the bat to put together a team of supporters who can carry the vision for their ministry. We don't demand that our young evangelists have 100% of their support before they start with us. It usually takes about two years to grow a group of financial supporters to the point where someone can have a full-time salary. This is why we encourage our new evangelists to keep their secular jobs, at least on a part-time basis, so that the financial burden doesn't become too overwhelming. As their support increases, they can begin to carve out more time for their ministry.

We also give them tools to help them get the word out on what's going on in their ministry: Websites, newsletters, prayer bulletins. The more widely their ministry is known, the quicker they can put together a team of supporters.

How can I go about developing a training program for budding evangelists in my local church?

The first step is to put together a hub of evangelists in your church (cf. Chapter 6). Rubbing shoulders with one's peers is an excellent learning tool. It is the responsibility of the local church to recognize those who have the gift of the evangelist and to confer them with authority so that they can begin to fulfill their ministry among the saints.

The second step is to put these evangelists in contact with movements or organizations who specialize in evangelistic ministry. The National Council of French Evangelists recommends sending budding evangelists to the European Evangelist's Forum every year. This provides them with a much needed time of spiritual reflection and encouragement:

- Training to develop the evangelist's skill set
- Networking which encourages the young evangelist to take advantage of available resources in the French-speaking evangelical world

You might also think about entrusting your budding evangelist to a group which will invest in his ministry without removing him from the local sphere. This is the case with FE, as we encourage involvement with the "network of associates" to develop the ministry of preaching evangelists.

How can we especially encourage the women in our churches that are gifted as evangelist?

You've touched upon a delicate subject which, in my opinion, has not been handled correctly in our local churches! So many female evangelists are not recognized as such because of the confusion between office and function. It is unfair and we regret this sad state of affairs. Where are the Becky Pipperts and the modern-day Jeanne Saillens?

But even as we recognize this inequality in our churches, we need not despair! At FE we've trained more than fifteen women in evangelistic ministry in the past five years. Women need to be, even more so than men, reassured as to the legitimacy of their ministry and taught how to practice it in a world that is often hostile to their efforts. Men, we need to give them a little room!

Martin Sanders, who wrote *The Power of Mentoring,* has consecrated a great amount of time and energy to training women in evangelism. His next book is dedicated to developing women leaders and will be an extremely useful tool for local churches.

CONCLUSION

DIARY OF A YOUNG EVANGELIST

Philippe Monnery

Christmas 1999: I'm attending a ski camp with my youth group in the heart of the French Alps, near Chambery. The speaker is a guy from German-speaking Switzerland. He speaks French, but I can hardly understand a word he says. Except this one phrase that he keeps repeating over and over: "Let's change our lives in the year 2000!" It makes me laugh because it's the same phrase that one of the major grocery store chains is using in their commercials.

Why should I change? I've been going to church since I was a little kid; I've heard it all. I've even prayed several times, "Lord, I'm a sinner; I believe you died on the cross for me. Save me." So what do I need to change? I'm a Christian, what's the problem?

I'm feeling down. My life is boring. So what if I know the Bible back and forth, all the stories from Adam to Paul. At the end of the day, it's all just theoretical. The fact of the matter is that none of it has anything to do with my life. I'm feeling lost… helpless.

There's the Sunday Philippe and the weekday Philippe; the Philippe who knows his Bible almost by heart, and the Philippe who lies and steals. The Philippe who says he knows Jesus, and yet takes his name in vain.

I can talk the talk, but it doesn't matter; I know I'm far from God. I'm hanging around with people who are leading me down the wrong path, and my sin is controlling me. I know all about Jesus, but I don't know him.

A still small voice in my head is whispering, "This has got to change!" Alone in my room, I open the Bible my aunt gave me a few years back, and I read this passage from the book of Proverbs:

> "My son, if sinners entice you, do not consent. If they say, 'Come with us [...] my son, do not walk in the way with them; hold back your foot from their paths, for their feet run to evil, and they make haste to shed blood'" (Proverbs 1:10-16).

I realize how far I really am from God. My feet run towards evil and I know that I'm heading straight for God's judgment. A deep conviction of sin comes over me and I get down on my knees before the God who gave his Son for me.

Autumn 2000: My first steps as a baby Christian ... I spend a lot of my time witnessing to my unsaved friends. God changed my life and I want to tell others about it.

I read Hudson Taylor's biography, after finding it on my parents' bookshelf. His life is such an inspiration to me: His faith, his zeal, his heart for lost people. A lot of his letters appear in the book, and a few lines from one of them really touch my heart:

> "Souls are perishing on all sides because they do not know the truth. How can we sit here, doing nothing, while the blood of the nations falls upon our heads?"

These words really hit me hard. The mission field is vast, and I want to be a part of it. I want to give my life to it… all my life.

A couple of weeks later, I'm part of an evangelistic camp in Chambery. We've just finished a street performance and a young man is standing in front of me, tears running down his face. The message of the Gospel that we portrayed in our performance really touched his heart. I take a few minutes to talk to him about what God wants to do in his life, if he'll just open his heart to him.

Several days after the camp, I tell my mom, "Mom, I want to be a missionary!" She looks at me, surprised. I find out later that she has been praying for years that I would give my whole life to God.

Spring 2004: God continues to work in my life. I've been preaching in my church for two years now. I've had the privilege of participating in several evangelistic crusades and I've been ministering at a Christian youth camp on weekends and during school breaks, where I've had the joy of leading several people to Christ. My desire to serve him is still there.

I decide that I want to go to Bible school, as soon as I get my high school diploma. But sadly, this doesn't work out. So, at the start of the next school year, I start my university studies in mathematics, in the city of Saint-Etienne. I'm still preaching at church, but I don't have time now to work at the youth camp. I feel like I'm going around in circles. Some of my friends and I decide to start up a group where we can organize street evangelism in our city and other cities in the area, working with youth groups from several churches. Through these events, I get to know other Christians in different churches in the area.

Little by little, our evangelistic efforts start to grow, and I want to encourage other young evangelists to step up to the plate. So I decide to organize a week-long evangelistic camp where we can train young people and reach a part of our city for Christ. I start looking for others to help out at the camp, and I meet Raphael Anzenberger, who is an evangelist with a mission called France Evangelization. After talking for five minutes, he agrees to be our camp speaker.

Spring 2006: Our first evangelistic camp is over. We saw God work in a powerful way! Many people were touched by the Gospel. God opened doors for us to witness in several different public venues, including the town's movie theater. The young people who came to the camp went back home encouraged.

As Raphael is getting ready to head home, he mentions that he is working on starting up a network of young evangelists, and he'd like me to be a part of the network. Could this be the start of something important in my life?

Several months later, I arrive in Touraine four hours before the beginning of the launch weekend of R2E. I have no idea what will take place during the weekend, but the program looks amazing. For the very first time, I'm going to meet up with other young evangelists, and we'll be accompanied by our mentor, Alain Stamp.

Summer 2008: I finish the R2E training program, and my vision for ministry is stronger than ever. I feel that I've obtained a solid foundation for future service. I have more confidence now in God's calling on my life and I'm encouraged by my relationships with other evangelists and with my mentors. During the second year of R2E, we were encouraged to work on our ministry development plan, and I'm eager for everything to fall into place.

My ministry continues to grow and I become an associate evangelist with France Evangelization. I've been organizing evangelistic camps for four years now in Saint-Etienne, and other churches are starting to invite me to preach on Sundays. The love of Christ constrains me.

My college diploma in hand, I find a job in commercial engineering. Several people have advised me to get some work experience before jumping into the ministry full-time. I really want to be a testimony at work, but it doesn't work out that way. The harvest doesn't come, and I find myself constantly busy with meetings. I feel like I'm up against a wall in my job, yet at the same time, churches continue to ask me to preach. I don't understand what's going on ... I'm confused.

Autumn 2010: Alain, Raphael, Saotra (a friend I met during my R2E training) and I leave for Cape Town for the Third Lausanne Conference for World Evangelization. I realize anew the vastness of the mission field, as well as the zeal burning in the hearts of the evangelists surrounding me. I hear tell of God's greatness as He accompanies these men and women in their ministry. This is my dream: to give my life for Christ as I take the Gospel to the ends of the earth. I remember Hudson Taylor…

Spring 2011: The local church continues to grow, and I take on more responsibilities there. Between my involvement at church and outside invitations, I'm preaching up to three times a week, besides my full-time job. I'm feeling exhausted, and it's getting hard to keep up. My family is feeling it too, as we have just had our first child. My schedule is too crazy; something's got to give. The love of Christ burns in my heart: I see people giving their lives to Him and I want more than ever to invest in full-time ministry. Lord, what do you really want me to do?

No one can make this decision for me; I've got to step out in faith. I decide to take the risk and send in my application for part-time ministry as an evangelist with France Evangelization.

Winter 2011: I continue to work at my engineering job. It doesn't look like my aspiration to work as a part-time evangelist is going to work out. Although I can't start part-time with France Evangelization, I'm still convinced that God is working things out. He's proven it to me over and over again. I'm doing well spiritually, but I'm really tired. For months now, I've been working full-time and ministering many hours per week. I feel stressed, burdened. It's a dark time for me.

Like every year, the moment comes for the annual Evangelistic Forum. This year it is to be held in Belgium. But, I'm so down, I don't even feel like going. I drag myself to the Forum, where Stephen Lungu is the speaker. I enjoy getting back in touch with friends, but I don't feel any encouragement from the messages. I feel empty and incapable of getting back on my feet. But, despite my fatigue, God has prepared something for me.

During the closing message, Stephen Lungu talks about how God prepares us for ministry. He speaks of the dark times, the waiting, the feelings of despair, and the success of others – all these spiritual disciplines that God uses to forge the character of his servants. This man, who lives at the other end of the earth, is describing my life to a T!

Broken, touched by God's love, I go back home. I'm exhausted, but restored! A sunbeam is peeking through my dark clouds. God is in control of my ministry.

Spring 2012: The flame is burning brighter than ever and my wife and I both have a renewed conviction in our hearts. God is calling us to follow Him by faith. I am convinced that I should leave my secular job, and that He will take care of the rest.

I meet with my boss in order to explain my project to him. I'm surprised to hear him congratulate me and we agree to separate on good terms. In the weeks to come, God confirms our decision over and over again. Doors open for financial support and for us to announce the Gospel full-time.

As I look back, I remember those eleven years since God first called me to follow Him. Eleven years of joy, of victory and of learning. Eleven years of questions, of battles and of frustration. Eleven years of darkness, of waiting, of feeling uncomfortable where I was, of watching other succeed in what I desired to do.

Eleven years which taught me this: when Christ calls someone, He really calls them. But, He must be our motivation; we dare not depend on our circumstances. His discipline in my life is not there to disqualify me, but rather to teach me to lean more on Him so that I can fly ever higher.

God cannot use me until the ministry is no longer my project, but His project.

Philippe Monnery

I love Philippe's story.

At 25 years of age, he represents a new generation of young people who wish to consecrate their lives to world evangelism. These are the Hudson Taylors of today.

Dr. Bill Jones, mentor and professor of evangelism at Columbia International University, often told me: "Don't worry about the size of your ministry, but rather about the depth of your relationship with Christ. The impact of your ministry will come from the depths of your closeness to Jesus." That's why I rejoice (secretly) when I see our young evangelists go through times of discouragement, of waiting, of restlessness, of being jealous of others' successes. I just remind myself that God hasn't finished calling… some as evangelists.

Raphaël Anzenberger

ASKING THE TOUGH QUESTIONS[1]

1. ***Blessed are the poor in spirit*** *(Matthew 5:1-3).*
   - Are you proud?
   - Do you brag about yourself?
   - Do you put your desires above Christ's?

2. ***Blessed are those who morn*** *(Matthew 5:4).*
   - Do you have a lack of concern for people's needs?
   - Are you apathetic about sin?
   - Have you lost your desire to see your friends come to Christ?

3. ***Blessed are the gentle*** *(Matthew 5:5).*
   - Have you been insensitive to the emotional needs of others?
   - Are you rude and uncaring?
   - Do you intentionally hurt people's feelings?

4. ***Blessed are those who hunger and thirst for righteousness*** *(Matthew 5:6).*
   - Have you wanted to be happy more than holy?
   - Have you lost your desire to be godly?
   - Have you lacked concern about walking righteously?

[1]Excerpts taken from *Without Blame* by Dr. Bill Jones. ©1992 Crossover Communications International. Used by permission.

5. ***Blessed are the merciful*** *(Matthew 5:7).*
   - Is there anyone to whom you have not shown mercy?
   - Do you enjoy making others suffer?
   - Have you failed to be kind to those less fortunate?

6. ***Blessed are the pure in heart*** *(Matthew 5:8).*
   - Have your motives been impure?
   - Have you manipulated others?
   - Have you wanted to be recognized by others?

7. ***Blessed are the pure in heart*** *(Matthew 5:9).*
   - Do you fuss and fight with your family or friends?
   - Do you always try to have the last word?
   - Are you reluctant to say, "I'm sorry"?

8. ***Blessed are those who have been persecuted for the sake of righteousness... Rejoice and be glad...*** *(Matthew 5:10-12).*
   - Have you been ashamed of Christ?
   - Have you avoided standing up for Him?
   - Have you complained about persecution?

9. ***Let your light shine before men in such a way that they may see your good works*** *(Matthew 5:13-16).*
   - Are there friends that don't know you are a Christian?
   - Have you tried to be one of the crowd?
   - Have you failed to tell others that Christ is why you act as you do?

10. ***Whoever then annuls one of the least of these commandments and so teaches others, shall be called least in the kingdom of heaven*** *(Matthew 5:17-20).*
    - Have you considered any of God's Word as unimportant?
    - Do you justify any of your actions that disregard God's Word?
    - Have you led others astray by your disobedience?

11. ***Everyone who is angry with his brother shall be guilty before the court*** *(Matthew 5:21-26).*
    - Are you easily angered?
    - Are there people you are mad with now?
    - Have you said things to intentionally hurt another?

12. ***Everyone who looks on a woman to lust for her has committed adultery with her already in his heart*** *(Matthew 5:27-32).*
    - Have your eyes been lustful?
    - Do you have any impure habits?
    - Are you involved in any immoral relationships?

13. ***Let your statement be "yes, yes" or "no, no"; and anything beyond these is of evil*** *(Matthew 5:33-37).*
    - Has your word been undependable?
    - Have you been irresponsible?
    - Have you failed to follow through on your commitments?

14. ***Whoever slaps you on your right cheek, turn to him the other also*** *(Matthew 5:38-42).*
    - Are you quick to get revenge?
    - Do you always want to get even?
    - Have you failed to give others a "second chance"?

15. ***Love your enemies and pray for those who persecute you*** *(Matthew5:43-48).*
    - Do you hate anyone?
    - Have you failed to pray for those who persecute you?
    - Have you failed to do good to those who do bad to you?

16. ***Beware of practicing your righteousness before men to be noticed by them*** *(Matthew 6:1).*
    - Do you try to impress people?
    - Do you have to be the center of attention?
    - Do you do "spiritual" things just so others will notice?

17. ***When you give alms*** *(Matthew 6:2-4).*
    - Have you failed to tithe?
    - Do you give begrudgingly?
    - Have you failed to give sacrificially?

18. ***When you pray*** *(Matthew 6:5-13).*
    - Do you think about other things when people pray?
    - Are your prayers insincere?
    - Do you actually pray when you tell someone that you will?

19. ***If you forgive men of their transgressions, your Heavenly Father will also forgive you*** *(Matthew 6:14-15).*
    - Are you resentful of anyone?
    - Are you holding any grudges?
    - Do you remind others of past offenses?

20. ***Whenever you fast*** *(Matthew 6:16-18).*
    - Have you failed to fast?
    - Do your appetites control you?
    - Do you let others know when you're fasting?

21. ***Do not lay up for yourself treasures upon earth*** *(Matthew 6:19-21).*
    - Are there things more important to you than God?
    - Do you have any possessions that you idolize?
    - Have you failed to lay up treasure in heaven?

22. ***The lamp of the body is the eye, if therefore your eye is clear, your whole body will be full of light*** *(Matthew 6:22-23).*
    - Are you envious of anyone or covetous of anything?
    - Have you been watching any sensual programs or movies?
    - Have you been reading ungodly magazines?

23. ***Do not be anxious*** *(Matthew 6:25-32).*
    - Are you a worrier?
    - Are you concerned about your needs being met?
    - Have you failed to trust God for His provisions?

24. ***Seek first His kingdom and His righteousness*** *(Matthew 6:33,34).*
    - Has God slipped from first place in your life?
    - Have you failed to give God your focused attention on a daily basis?
    - Have you let unconfessed sin linger in your life?

25. ***Do not judge lest you be judged yourself*** *(Matthew 7:1-6).*
    - Have you judged others?
    - Do you look down on anybody?
    - Do you have a "holier than thou" attitude?

26. ***Ask... Seek... Knock*** *(Matthew 7:7-11).*
    - Have you neglected to pray each day?
    - Do you pray more for yourself than for others?
    - Have you overlooked thanking God for His answers?

27. ***Whatever you want others to do for you, do so for them*** *(Matthew 7:12).*
    - Have you neglected serving others?
    - Have you focused more on yourself than on others?
    - Are you choosy about whom you serve?

28. ***Enter by the narrow gate*** *(Matthew 7:13-14).*
    - Have you refused to do what is right when it has been hard?
    - Have you failed to stand up for Christ?
    - Do you let others persuade you to do things that are wrong?

29. ***Every tree that does not bear good fruit is cut down and thrown into the fire*** *(Matthew 7:15-20).*
    - Is it hard for people to see Christian fruit in your life?
    - Have love, joy, peace and patience been absent from your life?
    - What about kindness, goodness, faithfulness, gentleness and self-control?

30. ***Not everyone who says to me, "Lord, Lord," will enter the kingdom of heaven; but he who does the will of my Father who is in heaven*** *(Matthew 7:21-22).*
    - Are there any areas in your life in which you are deliberately disobeying God?
    - Are you afraid to give Christ total control of your life?
    - Are you the boss of your life?

31. ***Everyone who hears these words of mine and acts upon them, may be compared to a wise man who built his house upon the rock*** *(Matthew 7:24-29).*
    - Do you hear God's word and fail to do it?
    - Do you act as if God's Word is unimportant?
    - Have you failed to read God's Word each day?

BIBLIOGRAPHY

Doctoral Thesis

ANZENBERGER, Raphaël. *Formative evaluation of R2E: mentoring a new generation of evangelists for France* [Thèse de doctorat]. Columbia (USA): Columbia international university, 2011.

Qualifications of the Evangelist

BUCHHOLD, Jacques. "Évangéliste." In *Dictionnaire de théologie pratique*. Charols: Excelsis, 2011.

CARSWELL, Roger. *L'Évangéliste: Un ministère à découvrir*. Saint-Légier: Emmaüs, 2009.

OLFORD, Stephen. The evangelist's gift and ministry. In Douglas, John (ed.). *The work of an evangelist*, p. 143-150. Minneapolis: World Wide Publications, 1983.

PARZANY, Ulrich. The gift and calling of the evangelist. In Conard W. (ed.). *The mission of an evangelist*, p. 23-30. Minneapolis: World Wide Publications, 2000.

SANDERS, Martin, STAMP, Alain. *Multiplier les leaders: Le mentorat, l'art de l'accompagnement*. Marpent: BLF, 2011.

The Personsal Life of the Evangelist

BOUNDS, Edward M. *The Complete works of E. M. Bounds on prayer.* Grand Rapids: Baker Books, 2000.

JOHNSTONE, Patrick, MANDRYCK, Jason. *Flashes sur le monde francophone.* Dijon: Éditions missionnaires francophones, 2006.

ORTBERG, John. *The Life You've Always Wanted.* Grand Rapids (USA): Zondervan Publishing House, 1997.

Conference Publications

CONARD, W. (ed.). *The mission of an evangelist.* Minneapolis: World Wide Publications, 2001. Actes du congrès d'Amsterdam 2000, dont ces contributions:
- FINKENBINDER, Paul. The evangelist relies on the Holy Spirit, p. 147-156;
- GRAHAM, Billy, RADZIZEWSKI, Bruno. The evangelist and prayer, p. 157-158;
- BRIGHT, Bill et Vonette. The evangelist and prayer, p. 159-166;
- GRAHAM, Franklin. The evangelist's heart of compassion, p. 167-174;
- OLFORD, Stephen. The evangelist's inner life, p. 183-190;
- RAINEY, Dennis. The evangelist's family, p. 193-200.

DOUGLAS, J. (ed.). *The calling of an evangelist: The second international congress for itinerant evangelists, Amsterdam, the Netherlands.* Minneapolis: World Wide Publications, 1987, 430 p. Actes du congrès d'Amsterdam 1986, dont ces contributions:
- FORD, Leighton. The evangelist's strength in weakness, p. 19-24;
- GRAHAM LOTZ, Anne. The evangelist's faithfulness, p. 39-42;
- KRIESE, Richard. The prayer time of the evangelist;
- OLFORD, Stephen. The evangelist and the personal life of holiness, p. 3-14;
- SWEETING, George. The evangelist's passion for the lost, p. 35-38;
- TCHIVIDJIAN, Stephan. Your inner life as an evangelist, p. 77-84.

DOUGLAS, J. (ed.). *The work of an evangelist: International congress for itinerant evangelists, Amsterdam, The Netherlands, 1983.* Minneapolis: World Wide Publications, 1984. Actes du congress Amsterdam 1983, dont ces contributions:
- BARROWS, Cliff. The evangelist and his family: We manage our own families well, p. 55-64;
- BRIGHT, Bill. The evangelist's personal witness, p. 25-34;
- CHO, Paul Yong-Gi. The evangelist and the life of faith: We walk by faith, not sight, p. 19-28;
- FORD, Leighton. The evangelist and the great commission: We preach to the ends of the world, p. 65-72;
- GRAHAM LOTZ, Anne. The evangelist and the life of prayer: We labor in prayer, p. 29-34;
- GREEN, Michael. The evangelist and spiritual freshness of life: We press on toward the mark, p. 47-54;
- HILL, Edward. The evangelist and the glory of God: We magnify his name, p. 19-28;
- PALAU, Luis. The evangelist and his personal life: We are called to be holy, p. 11-18.